BRAZZÀ,
A LIFE FOR AFRICA

by

Maria Petringa

Bloomington, IN   Milton Keynes, UK
         authorHOUSE

AuthorHouse™
1663 Liberty Drive, Suite 200
Bloomington, IN 47403
www.authorhouse.com
Phone: 1-800-839-8640

AuthorHouse™ UK Ltd.
500 Avebury Boulevard
Central Milton Keynes, MK9 2BE
www.authorhouse.co.uk
Phone: 08001974150

© *2006 Maria A. Petringa. All Rights Reserved.*

No part of this book may be reproduced, stored in a retrieval system, or transmitted by any means without the written permission of the author.

First published by AuthorHouse 01/13/06

ISBN: 1-4259-1198-6 (sc)

Library of Congress Control Number: 2005911347

Printed in the United States of America
Bloomington, Indiana

"The truth is behind the mountains.
To find it, you must travel."

-- Senegalese proverb

This book is dedicated to the children of Africa.

TABLE OF CONTENTS

List of Illustrations		ix
Preface		xi
Foreword by Lucia Pirzio-Biroli,		
an American descendant of Brazzà		xvii

One	The Count of Brazzà	1
Two	*Le Cartahu*	12
Three	The Ensign	27
Four	The Father of Slaves	37
Five	The Barefoot Conqueror	58
Six	The Explorer	84
Seven	The Challenger	95
Eight	The Toast of Paris	110
Nine	The General Commissioner	129
Ten	The Diplomat	148
Eleven	*Rocamambo*	158
Twelve	The Bridegroom	172
Thirteen	The Father	184
Fourteen	The Investigator	198
Fifteen	Honored Son of France	218

Conclusion	230
Brazzà's Paris	233
Notes	235
About the Research	241
Bibliography	244

LIST OF ILLUSTRATIONS

All images courtesy of the
Bibliothèque Nationale de France, Paris.

1. Brazzà, an Ensign in the French Navy, about 1875   29

2. A Friday evening at *la Petite Vache*   32

3. Brazzà about 1882 (A detail of this photograph appears on the cover.)   127

4. Dr. Noël Ballay in 1886   140

5. Charles de Chavannes about 1890   141

6. Brazzà with an African chief around 1890   166

7. Brazzà in 1905   199

PREFACE

A century ago, a biography of Pierre Savorgnan de Brazzà would have been superfluous, at least in Europe, because the Franco-Italian explorer was a major figure on the late 19th-century cultural, political, and social scene. Colonialism was at its height, and each time Brazzà, a tall, dark, and handsome naval officer, returned to Paris after a few years exploring uncharted Africa, he was given a hero's welcome. He was photographed and written about, Parisians smoked Brazzà cigarettes in his honor, and to this day many cafés in Paris are named *Le Brazza* after him. He was asked to London to speak about his discoveries to the Royal Societies of Geography and Natural History. In Italy, where he was born, he held the title of count of one of Italy's oldest noble families. His explorations in the name of France were a main topic of discussion at Bismarck's Berlin Conference of 1884 on colonial policy in Africa.

Nowadays even a Frenchman would be hard-pressed to remember Brazzà's life and achievements. The charismatic explorer died in Dakar under mysterious circumstances in 1905, at the relatively early age of 53. After giving him an elaborate state funeral, the French government decided to obscure Brazzà's accomplishments, despite the considerable slice of Africa he had claimed for France, his adopted country. The explorer's fame survives only in the hearts of Africans, and in the name of Brazzaville, one of the cities he founded, now the capital of the Republic of the Congo.

It was while I was living in Brazzaville years ago that I became interested in his unusual story. Brazzà's memory is venerated by the Congolese, who staunchly refuse to change the name of Brazzaville, unlike residents of virtually all other former European colonies on the continent, who immediately restored their cities' African names at the time of national independence. While doing my shopping in the Congolese capital, I would occasionally see framed photographs of Brazzà on store and office walls.

I was intrigued by this seeming paradox: Brazzà was forgotten by the French, who had profited largely from his explorations, yet revered by the Africans, whom he had governed as a colonial administrator for a faraway foreign power. To satisfy my own curiosity, I sought details of the explorer's life, but found little. Years later, deep in the bowels of France's research libraries, I located four or five books on Brazzà which helped me to solve the mystery. I learned that Brazzà had, in all likelihood, been poisoned for his attempts to improve the lot of the Africans under French colonial rule. Like Dreyfus, he had been an innocent victim of 19th-century corruption and prejudice. Besides my personal fascination with the man, his explorations, and his tragic destiny, I felt a moral duty to make Brazzà's story known.

By turns a diplomat, a conqueror, a humanitarian, and an anthropologist, Brazzà forged himself a life that was unique and compelling. While he shared the courage and enthusiasm of more familiar figures such as Livingstone,

Lewis and Clark, and Amelia Earhart, he never fit the mold of the typical European explorer in Africa who accomplished his ends through violent means, as did Henry Morton Stanley and many others. Brazzà's attempts to understand African culture "from the inside," that is, by living among the tribes and patiently learning their ways, and his successful use of diplomacy, were quite revolutionary. His confrontation with the corrupt and racist French colonial administration is a universal story of a man who remained faithful to his ideology, even at the cost of his life. His unshakeable opposition to slavery makes him, with his contemporary Abraham Lincoln, an ancestor of the Civil Rights Movement.

At the same time, Brazzà was a skilled negotiator who knew how to charm and convince people in order to achieve his ends. Some of his statements, as well as his actions, were contradictory, and his true motivations sometimes seem obscure. Several of his most faithful colleagues occasionally found him unreasonable and stubborn, and admitted that they could not understand the intense personal vision that guided his life and work. Brazzà's untimely death at the age of 53 prevented him from writing his memoirs, and a systematic history of his explorations has never been compiled. Thus Brazzà remains a mysterious figure.

In establishing French sovereignty over a large part of west central Africa, Brazzà played a key role in the dramatic events of the colonial period, an era that defined many aspects of modern-day life on the continent. Most African nations' current boundaries, their official languages, educational systems, religious institutions, transportation networks, and even the crops, minerals, and other products that provide their income were largely determined by the colonial powers. For better or worse, colonialism played a pivotal role in

Africa's development, and a thorough knowledge of the forces at work during this time is essential to an understanding of contemporary Africa.

The sweeping changes and catastrophic events of the colonial era were brought about, not by stereotypical villains and heroes, but by a vast number of ordinary human beings for a wide variety of reasons and motivations, some noble, some ignoble. Each actor in this significant human drama deserves to be known and evaluated on his or her own merits. I hope that the 21st century will bring forth a long-overdue attempt by Americans and others to come to know African history and culture as it really is and was, not as we imagine it to be. I intend this biography as an aid to those who want to learn about the African continent, not as a bone of contention, a reminder of a guilty past, or an object of condescension, but as a land with a fascinating past and a vibrant, viable future.

Brazzà, A Life for Africa is the result of years of research in libraries and archives too numerous to name here (although a note about my research path and a detailed bibliography appear at the end of this book). I would like to express my appreciation, however, to the helpful staff of the Bibliothèque Mazarine and the Bibliothèque Nationale de France, both in Paris, and the Archives Nationales d'Outre-Mer in Aix-en-Provence. I note my admiration of, and pride in, the Library of Congress in Washington, D. C., which I consider the world's standard in reference institutions.

I am indebted to many people for invaluable encouragement, advice, and support. By their unfailing interest and faith in Brazzà's story and in my ability to tell it, *Harvard Magazine* editor Jean Martin and screenwriter Debbie Danielpour Chapel helped bring about the genesis of this book. Stephen Provencal, Dr. Carroll Yoder, Carl Cockburn, and Virginie Batchy shared their knowledge of Africa, took the time to read all or part of my manuscript, and offered excellent suggestions. Dr. Jean Pedersen and Katherine Lee advised me on French history and politics, and also read and commented on sections of the manuscript. Dr. Valerie Abrahamsen, Pat Clark, Lora Berg, Mary Postizzi, Jaylene Sarracino, and Dr. Jerome Singerman guided me on my way into the world of publishing.

Cristiana Rabusin provided me with an introduction to the grandnephew of Pierre Savorgnan de Brazzà, Dr. Detalmo Pirzio-Biroli, a professor of African history and a consultant on international development. As the present Count of Brazzà, he welcomed me into his home, the Castello di Brazzà near Udine, Italy. Detalmo's enthusiasm and encouragement, as well as his extensive family memorabilia and his recollections of conversations with the explorer's wife Thérèse, were an inestimable aid to my work.

Lucia Pirzio-Biroli, Brazzà's American great-grandniece, contacted me in 2003 and since then has provided unwavering support for the biography. Despite her busy schedule, she has taken the time to advise me on many aspects of her family history.

Further research assistance was cheerfully given by Annick Ribère-Magen, Dr. Fabian Schupper, and Jason Davis. Joël Souamy made available his exceptional photographs of traditional life in Gabon. For their loyal support and congeniality during the "long winter of the last draft," I send my heartfelt thanks to writer Ellen Bomer, screenwriter Andrea Bempensante, and historical researcher Robin Whitmore.

January 25, 2002, marked the sesquicentennial anniversary of Pierre Savorgnan de Brazzà's birth, and September 14, 2005 marks the centennial of his death. I hope that readers will find my account of his extraordinary life entertaining and informative, and that the biography will stimulate enlightened reflection on Africa's manifold relations with the rest of the world.

Maria Petringa
Paris, September 2005

Comments about this book may be sent to <brazza.bio@gmail.com>.

FOREWORD

by Lucia Pirzio-Biroli,
an American descendant of Brazzà

It is with anticipation that I await the publication of this biography of Pietro Savorgnan di Brazzà. This engagingly written, impeccably researched book is an opportunity to revive the nearly lost story of a man who stood his ground against the rising tide of colonial Europe. There are always two sides to the same history, and Pietro's life is that other side. It is a story so fascinating, with an arc so grand, and so full of real adventure and heroism, that it is difficult to imagine it could all fit into such a brief and brilliant lifetime. And yet today, a hundred years after his death, in a time when the hubris of power has reached another chilling crescendo, Pietro's story of quiet courage stands as an example of respect for the dignity of all humanity.

As Pietro's descendant, I know his story as part of our family's oral history. My relatives and I have heard it throughout our lifetimes. His ethos is deeply ingrained in our birthright. His ancestral home, Castello di Brazzà in northeastern Italy, is still in the family. My Italian cousins are friends with descendants of members of Pietro's exploration team, who also reside in their family home in a nearby town.

My Uncle Detalmo's library, animated with artifacts from his own academic and diplomatic career spent in Africa, features several photos of Pietro.

And yet there is so little published documentation that it is difficult to convey Pietro's greatness to those who haven't shared this cultural legacy retold during family gatherings. A few years ago, while gathering material for a notebook for my young nephew, to explain to him who this ancestor of his was who bought slaves and set them free, I came across Maria Petringa's 1997 one-page brief life of Pietro. It was the only material in English I could find, and along with copies of photos, a trip to the local zoo to see a "DeBrazza's Monkey," and our annotated family tree, it sparked an interest in the boy, gave him pride in his ancestry, and started a discussion on human rights.

The article on Pietro's life also inspired my meeting with Maria in 2003, and the beginning of our friendship and exchange of ideas on the importance of Pietro's legacy. I look forward to this book so that others, like my nephew, can come to know this inspiring and humble man.

Lucia Pirzio-Biroli
Seattle, September 2005

CHAPTER ONE -- THE COUNT OF BRAZZÀ

A pack of French cigarillos, and a familiar brand of Congolese cigarettes. An incongruous statue of a white man in Franceville, Gabon. The names of bars, cafés, and a few hotels all over France. A small residential street near Paris' military training school. A Roman square near the Trevi Fountain. A high school in Algiers. The capital city of the Republic of Congo. All these elements bear the name of Pierre Savorgnan de Brazzà, a 19th-century explorer whose evanescent fame owed more to his myth than his eventful personal history.

He came from an ancient and noble Italian family. He was adored by his mother, his wife, his children, and at one time by much of Europe. He was despised by French politicians, a Belgian King, a Welsh explorer, and many greedy rubber speculators. His memory is still honored by several African nations.

Gabriel Hanotaux, a former French Minister of Foreign Affairs, described Brazzà in his memoirs. "I can still see him, entering my office like a gust of wind ... thin, hairy, a bit stooped, with a shaggy beard and those warm, kind eyes. To us skeptical Parisians he looked like a prophet out of the wilderness. Beneath his delicate appearance, he was a man of precision, energy, and untiring perseverance, and when in his hesitant speech, interrupted by silences and as many detours as an African trail, he slowly laid out his grand plans, when he lifted the veil that hid the African continent from everyone but him, when he put his finger on that wide, blank map of Africa and said 'That's where we should be heading,' coming from him it seemed so simple that you'd think all you had to do was follow him to make a success of it. ... This great friend of Africa won her over, I daresay, because he loved her."

"The arrival of Pierre de Brazzà was a very moving event," wrote the Italian naturalist Attilio Pecile, who accompanied the explorer's expedition to Gabon in 1883. "I tell you it brought tears to my eyes to see the welcome he got from the Blacks. News of his arrival spread quickly, and canoes came from everywhere, overloaded with tribesmen wanting to see him and greet him, shouting, 'Our father has returned! Our father has returned!' The Adouma [tribesmen] ... all came to shake his hand and kiss it."

Brazzà's secretary, Charles de Chavannes, was fascinated by the explorer's talent for patient diplomacy and his willingness to spend days or even weeks talking and negotiating with each chieftain. "[Brazzà] has a special method of dealing with people, at one moment quiet, sitting down, then suddenly loud, standing up in a crescendo of talk and gesticulation, sometimes bending down from his great height to draw some lines on the ground in the native fashion, to help them understand what he is saying."

Brazzà had his detractors, particularly in the French press. A writer who signed himself only as "Ultor" (Latin for "the Avenger"), published the following lines in 1896: "Monsieur Pierre Savorgnan de Brazzà is a fortunate man.

He is successful in all his undertakings, not only in what he does, but especially in what he doesn't do. Those who work hard in any endeavor in [French] Congo, without a thought for Monsieur de Brazzà, are amazed to see all the merit of their successful labor attributed to him. ... Absolute ruler of his dominion of French Congo for the past thirteen years, he has been named Commander of the Legion of Honor, [though] he is the only lieutenant in the French navy who has never sailed a ship. And the [Paris] Geographical Society has crowned him with every laurel wreath they have to bestow. ... He had the luck to come along at the right time, and the shrewdness to take credit for all the discoveries made in West Africa in the last twenty years."

Whether or not he came along "at the right time," Brazzà was born at a crossroads of European history, and into one of the world's great ages of discovery. Technology was beginning its reign, though the world still held many mysteries and many unexplored places. Modern ideas were beginning to be felt and heard in politics as well as the arts. Europe and Africa were discovering each other and entering into a relationship that would enrich and impoverish, link and divide, help and cripple both continents for the entire 20th century and beyond.

In the middle of the turbulent 19th century, the proud nations of Europe were suffering a profound identity crisis. The world was changing. As Marx and Engels published the *Communist Manifesto*, and as workers and intellectuals discovered socialist ideas, a wave of uprisings and revolutions spread through the Continent. Labor movements and cries for democracy challenged the ruling class, and even the most humble citizens began to claim a voice in their destiny. Revolts erupting in France, Germany, Italy, and elsewhere were brutally repressed, but the people persisted in their demands for equality. Soon parliaments were elected, and constitutions were written and ratified in nearly every European state and kingdom.

The distinguished Savorgnan di Brazzà family was suffering an identity crisis as well. For more than a thousand years they had been one of Italy's noblest and most storied families, tracing their name and lineage as far back as the Roman Emperor Septimus Severus. Their forbears had ruled Venice and fought in the Crusades. They had been ennobled in the Middle Ages, and possessed fertile lands in the Friuli region of northeastern Italy. As the Renaissance dawned, a lady of the family, Maria Savorgnan, had maintained a lively romantic correspondence with the Venetian scholar Pietro Bembo. The history of Italy, and indeed of Europe, could be read in their family tree.

Ascanio Savorgnan di Brazzà had led a life worthy of his ancestors. A talented artist, he had traveled widely in his youth, sailing east to Greece and Turkey, and to Egypt, where he sketched the pyramids. He had met the literati of London and studied with the great sculptor Canova in Rome. But of all his destinations, it was Paris he loved the best. In the salons of the French capital, he had spoken of art and politics with some of the finest minds of Europe. Ascanio saw Paris as the world's meeting place of ideas, and the center of all that was beautiful in life.

As the century progressed, Ascanio Savorgnan di Brazzà was troubled. The life he knew seemed to be coming to an end. Age-old dynasties like those of Milan, Florence, and Venice, and even the unquestioned authority of the Papal States, were giving way to a democratic revolution growing all around Europe. Italy was taking shape as a unified state for the first time, in a great resurgence of national spirit called the *Risorgimento*. Giuseppe Garibaldi and his thousand volunteer soldiers, the "Redshirts," were making their way from Piedmont to Sicily, striving to unite the various dominions in a new Italian republic. But unification was an idea that seemed anomalous to many residents of Italian city-states that had long considered themselves independent. Venice, for example, saw itself as the ideal state: prosperous, democratic, beautiful, well-organized, and a patron of the arts. Its citizens had proudly called themselves Venetian for more than a thousand years, and changing their loyalties to a vague entity called Italy gave them pause to consider.

Like many of his countrymen, Ascanio found it difficult to adapt to this new state of affairs, and to determine his family's place in it. He well understood the people's need for democracy -- in fact, he had always admired the "Liberty, Equality, Fraternity" motto of the French Revolution -- but he was not sure what would replace the immutable, traditional lifestyle that noble families like his had followed for so many generations. Amidst all the political turmoil, the European countries were taking advantage of their neighbors' instability to gain more territory and power. Austria had taken possession of the city of Venice and its surrounding provinces, including the ancestral domain of the Savorgnan family.

Ascanio had chosen to reside in Rome during the foreign domination of his homeland. He was granted Roman citizenship by the Holy See, and it was in the Eternal City that he met his wife, Giacinta Simonetti, daughter of a noble Venetian family that descended from Marco Polo. Giacinta shared Ascanio's love of art and his admiration for France. In 1835, the Count and Countess Savorgnan di Brazzà settled into a happy domestic life in Rome and began raising a family. Ascanio was named curator of the Capitoline Museum of classical art. They lived in a Roman palazzo on Via dell'Umiltà, near the Trevi Fountain, and spent vacations at their country home in the town of Castel Gandolfo, overlooking Lake Albano, along the ancient Appian Way.

It was against this background of domestic tranquility and dynamic political change that Giacinta presented Ascanio with their tenth child and seventh son, Pietro Paolo Camillo Francesco, born at Castel Gandolfo on January 25, 1852. Though she adored all her children, Giacinta would always feel a special love for Pietro. According to Italian legend, a seventh son was especially blessed.

Pietro's childhood was a happy one in this large and loving family. Ascanio and Giacinta were a liberal, cosmopolitan couple who raised their children with discipline but encouraged them to follow their dreams and interests. From the beginning Pietro loved nature and the outdoors, and in his reading he soon showed a preference for adventure novels. As for school, he made his way through his lessons as best he could. He genuinely loved to learn, but had little patience with copybooks and repetition, and above all with spending the day indoors. He was often punished for hiding adventure stories behind his Latin textbooks.

Pietro lived for the time he spent in the open air, sailing, exploring nature, and playing with animals. Outdoors, he was ready for anything and headed from one daredevil deed to another. He and his brothers loved to play "navy," building makeshift boats to sail on Lake Albano, near their country home at Castel Gandolfo. Giacinta would hear their shouts and laughter, with Pietro always in the lead when it came to daring exploits. She resigned herself to his nature, hoping that her seventh son was truly endowed with preternatural good luck that would keep him from serious injury.

Stories retold by the Savorgnan di Brazzà family emphasize the future explorer's intrepidity. It is said that as Pietro grew, he continued to devour tales of adventure, and by age eleven he yearned to be like the heroes of the books he loved. To be like them, he needed courage. An imaginative boy, he was often troubled by nightmares, and he avoided gloomy places like the deserted Castel Gandolfo cemetery. But a hero should not have fears, he thought to himself. He decided to spend the night in the cemetery to conquer his phobia. One summer night, he crept out of the house, made his way to the cemetery, and stretched out in its darkest corner. After all the excitement of his escape from home, Pietro had no trouble sleeping. The next morning he congratulated himself and felt like a hero. He had conquered the ghosts!

Another traditional story tells of a challenge that came the boy's way when he found traps set by poachers on his family's land. Pietro tried to free the game birds caught in the traps. When the poachers saw what he was doing, they loosed their enormous hunting hound to chase the boy away. Of course Pietro was frightened, but in a split second he decided to overcome this fear as well. He stood his ground. The dog growled at him, and came closer. Pietro and the dog stared each other directly in the eye for a few minutes until the dog desisted, and began sniffing his hand. Deep down, Pietro had always known that he had nothing to fear from nature and its creatures, and here was further proof.

One day Ascanio had some exciting news for his children. The Veneto and Friuli regions had been won back from the Austrians and would be incorporated into the new Kingdom of Italy. The family made a long-awaited trip to Ascanio's native Friuli, to meet their relatives and to see their ancestral homes at Brazzà and Soleschiano. The journey from Rome to the shores of the Adriatic was an adventure for Pietro and his brothers and sisters, since it was their first real trip anywhere. Pietro loved the northern Italian countryside and was fascinated by his relatives' stories of their ancestors. He learned that in the past, some Savorgnans had traveled as far as America and China, and that many years ago one family adventurer had returned from Africa with a couple of elephant tusks, now immortalized in the Savorgnan coat of arms.

The Castello di Brazzà had a more extensive library than Pietro's parents' collection in Rome, and here he found many volumes of travelers' tales, huge globes, and venerable atlases. He pored over the large maps, picturing in his mind the world's great mountains, rivers, oceans, and deserts. But some maps, he noticed, were incomplete. The heart of Africa was covered by a large white space marked "unknown territory." Who would be the first, he wondered, to sail to that mysterious land, explore its mountains and rivers, discover its strange and wonderful animals, and fill in this empty space? Would he, Pietro, be the family's next great adventurer?

In the changing world of the 1860s, anything seemed possible. After observing life forms around the globe, the naturalist Charles Darwin had published *The Origin of Species*, challenging long-held beliefs in the role of divine providence in nature. The United States was expanding westward, as cowboys rode the plains and prospectors panned for gold. In France, Jules Verne was publishing his series of

Extraordinary Journeys Across Worlds Known and Unknown, firing the imaginations of boys like Pietro.

The young count of Brazzà set his heart on a career in the navy, as a sailor and explorer of uncharted lands. Italy had a brilliant naval tradition, and Pietro admired the great Venetian, Genoese, and Florentine explorers like Marco Polo, Christopher Columbus, Amerigo Vespucci, John and Sebastian Cabot. But in the seeming chaos of the Risorgimento, Pietro's parents were of two minds about the new kingdom's politics. Ascanio and Giacinta often spoke to their son about France which, rightly or wrongly, they saw as a more stable democracy than Italy, and above all as the homeland of human rights. Influenced by his parents' admiration for France, Pietro began to take an interest in the French navy, sharing his enthusiasm with everyone around him.

Pietro was attending junior high school at the Jesuit College in Rome. Despite his average grades and imperfect attendance record, several of his instructors recognized his talents. The principal, Father Angelo Secchi, gave astronomy lessons and noticed the boy's rapt attention to all things concerning the stars, planets, and celestial navigation. Secchi asked Pietro if he was planning to pursue studies in science, and Pietro confided his cherished hope to become a sailor in the French navy. Bemused at a response so precise coming from a boy of thirteen, Father Secchi wished him luck.

One day the sunny Roman weather was too tempting, and Pietro was very late for school. "There you are!" said Father Secchi. "This morning I had a visit from a French admiral. If you hadn't been off playing truant, I could have introduced you!" Admiral Louis de Montaignac, the commander of the French fleet at Civitavecchia, north of Rome, was an avid astronomer. He had come to see Father Secchi to discuss some recent discoveries. Pietro was crestfallen -- until Secchi revealed that all was not lost. The admiral was still in Rome, staying at the Hotel Minerva, just a short walk from Pietro's home on Via dell'Umiltà. The priest added that he could arrange a meeting. Pietro excitedly ran home to tell his parents, and an appointment with the admiral was swiftly arranged.

Pietro's attempt to make an impression on the French admiral was partly comical. Having no gloves to wear with his suit, he had borrowed a pair of yellow gloves belonging to one of his sisters. But despite his adolescent awkwardness, he demonstrated the earnest devotion to his ideals, the readiness to assume responsibility, and the personal magnetism that were to stay with him all his life. The admiral recognized his potential and promised to help the boy achieve his goal of entering France's prestigious naval academy.

A few days later the Admiral de Montaignac met with Ascanio and Giacinta, who agreed to the idea of sending Pietro to board at the Collège Sainte Geneviève in Paris. It was a well-known Jesuit high school that prepared young men for the French military academies. The Savorgnans had a cousin living in Paris, the Duchess Fitz-James, who could look in on the boy. Montaignac would see to the practical details in Paris, and promised that he and his family would help Pietro in any way they could.

In Rome, there were many things to arrange before the young count's departure. Since Pietro was a member of a noble family who were citizens of the Papal States, even the Pope was asked to give his permission. Slowly but surely, everything was accomplished. Pietro could hardly believe it:

he was headed toward his dream in France, and he felt as if he were walking on air.

CHAPTER TWO -- *LE CARTAHU*

In 1866, as 14-year-old Pietro arrived at his boarding school in Paris, the capital was peaceful. Italy, Austria, and Prussia were at war, and the French army was involved in conflicts in Europe and even in Mexico, but there was no fighting on French soil. To Pietro's parents, Paris must have seemed safer than Rome itself. At that moment Garibaldi's Redshirts were fighting for control of the Papal States, hoping to make Rome the capital of the young Kingdom of Italy.

As a member of a noble Italian family, Pietro was welcomed at the Ecole Sainte Geneviève. The school had been opened by the Jesuits only in 1854, but already had a fine reputation for education and discipline. Pietro's classmates were mostly well-born French youths who were being prepared to attend the army academy at Saint-Cyr, the naval academy at Brest, or the equally prestigious Polytechnique, the military engineering academy. Named for the patron saint of Paris, the Ecole Sainte Geneviève was popularly known as the "Rue des Postes School" and had a large, well-appointed campus in the heart of the Latin Quarter. The school shared the Rue des Postes, a narrow, ancient street which had existed since Roman times, with other academies, convents, and seminaries. Then as now, the neighborhood teemed with booksellers, university students and intellectuals from the nearby Sorbonne, and clergy from all over the world, as well as a host of local tradesmen and laborers who saw to their practical needs. The roles of the upper and lower classes in European society were quite distinct, and the two groups lived in virtually separate worlds. Had Pietro been the son of a Roman or Parisian shopkeeper, the Ecole Sainte Geneviève, and for that matter the naval academy, would have been as inaccessible to him as they would have been to a well-born girl.

Paris was as beautiful as Pietro's father had described it -- a flourishing metropolis of splendid mansions, cafés, theaters, and monuments. Thanks to Baron Haussmann, the city's prefect and urban planner extraordinaire, the last dozen years had seen the transformation of the muddy fields and crumbling tenements of Paris into handsome residential neighborhoods. The boulevards, for years a colorful and rather rough-and-tumble circuit of theaters and dance halls, had become magnificent avenues where Parisians went strolling to see and be seen, and to attend Italian plays and Jacques Offenbach's lively operettas. The heart of the Right Bank was dominated by shops, offices, churches, and imposing government buildings like the City Hall and the new Supreme Court. Paris was alive with an endless stream of people and merchandise that were borne through the streets by horse-drawn carriages, or along the Seine by boats and barges.

On an island poised between the commerce and government of the Right Bank and the scholarly pursuits of the Left Bank stood the majestic Notre Dame cathedral, one of the many landmarks by which Pietro would learn to find his way in this new and rather overwhelming city. As the cupola of San Pietro had presided over Rome, the dome of the French Pantheon stood watch over the Latin Quarter. The colors of Pietro's world had changed from the earthen browns and tans of Rome to the grey stone and sky of Paris.

The city's distinctive beauty did not make the boy's adjustment to a new life and culture any easier. He missed the loving care of his family and the warmth of the gentle Roman climate. In Paris, the sun was rare, and it seemed to rain every day. Classrooms and dormitories at the Collège were chilly and damp. Pietro sensed a certain coldness in the people, too. The French seemed hesitant to joke and laugh as easily as the Italians did. Even the young boys at the boarding school behaved with a certain formality, and it would take Pietro a while to get used to their distant manner.

The French language was another chilling obstacle. Never a brilliant student, Pietro found French grammar and accents quite mysterious. His classmates taunted him for his errors in pronunciation. Used to being well-liked, Pietro was hurt and sad. This was the first serious difficulty he had ever encountered in his life, and now he did not even have his parents to turn to for encouragement. There were no more weekends spent roaming the idyllic countryside of Castel Gandolfo and playing games with his brothers. All he had were his mother's affectionate letters from home. As for skipping school when he was bored and restless, that too was a thing of the past. Unlike the teachers in Rome who had known his family personally and were willing to be a little indulgent, the Jesuits at Sainte Geneviève prided themselves on their discipline, and Pietro was kept busy for virtually every waking hour.

These lonely years in Paris were the first challenge of Pietro's young life, but for him there was only one possible response. He would set his mind to his work, and concentrate on his all-important goal of entering the naval academy. However long it took, he would do his best to learn the language and customs of this daunting yet fascinating land. During his free moments, Pietro buried himself in his beloved adventure stories. Soon he was able to read the thrilling tales of Jules Verne and Alexandre Dumas in the original French.

When Admiral de Montaignac was in Paris, he and his family would visit with Pietro, and kid him about the yellow gloves he had worn to their first meeting. Pietro's cousin, the duchess Fitz-James, would occasionally invite the boy to their home on the elegant Rue du Faubourg Saint Honoré. As time went on, Pietro made a few friends among his schoolmates and realized that quite a few of them were also far from their families. One boy named Dalin was from Lyon, and like Pietro he missed the warmer climate and the more relaxed southern lifestyle of his home town.

As Pietro matured he would come to accept the idiosyncrasies of Parisian life, and appreciate the intellectual and artistic ferment the city seemed to inspire and foster. In later years he would meet many of the distinguished people who came to the French capital to develop and share their ideas. Paris' Left Bank, where he now labored over mathematical exercises and Latin translations, was to be the scene of some of the most decisive events in Pietro's life.

In December 1868, one month shy of his seventeenth birthday, Pietro was admitted to the naval academy at Brest as a foreign student, placing 53rd in an admission class of 73. He was jubilant. His days as a schoolboy were over! Now he would wear a navy uniform and learn the practical skills that he needed to be a sailor.

At that time, the French naval academy did not occupy any buildings on land. It consisted of a training ship, the *Borda*, a three-masted warship that had seen action at the Battle of Sebastopol a dozen years earlier. The academy also possessed some smaller craft that were used for practical exercises. The young cadets lived right on the *Borda* where they slept in hammocks and were completely immersed in life at sea. Meals were austere and duties were regimented, but after all those years of Jesuit education, Pietro was used to discipline. He loved spending the day outdoors and learning all the practical details of life on board ship: hoisting the huge sails, climbing the masts, map-reading, navigating, mastering the variety of knots, and everything else that went into maintaining a sea-going vessel.

Although Pietro still had the Italian accent that he would never completely lose, he was now proficient in French and could express himself easily. On the *Borda*, of course, the students had a language of their own: a naval academy slang. The cadets called themselves *bordaches*. The commandant was referred to as "the Pope," and his second was known as "the Widow." Soon Pietro would be called *le cartahu*, a nickname of which he was very proud. It meant an agile, brave, adept naval cadet, to whom the duties of life at sea came easily: the ideal sailor.

Brest was not a beautiful city, and it had an even greyer and chillier climate than Paris, but Pietro appreciated the dramatic setting and the maritime feel of the place. It was the port city *par excellence*, perched above the Atlantic on the windswept western tip of Brittany, in a region known as Finistère, or "the end of the earth." On the *Borda*, Pietro lived in harmony with the rhythm of the waves, tides, and tempests. The Bretons' rugged, untamed Celtic nature seemed to respond to something in his own.

Among Pietro's shipmates on the *Borda* were several future notables. After a life at sea, Julien Viaud would achieve fame as Pierre Loti, author of immensely popular novels set in exotic places like Constantinople, Tahiti, and Japan. A year behind Pietro was Louis Mizon, later a commander in the Congo. The young Italian cadet made a number of friends, and impressed his shipmates with his skills, leadership, and optimism. Future naval captain Morazzani described Pietro as friendly and good-humored, even when he was teased about his Italian accent. Agile, strong, and an excellent swimmer, he well deserved the informal title of *le cartahu*. In difficult circumstances and on special occasions, Pietro was invariably placed at the helm of the ship. Future naval commandant Boyer, another classmate on the *Borda*, never forgot one particular incident. In the middle of a maneuver Boyer slipped and tumbled off the ship, and would have plunged into the icy water of the River Penfeld, had not Pietro managed to grab him and pull him to safety.

As the years passed Pietro came to love France, the country that was giving him the opportunity to fulfill his dream of becoming a sailor. Nevertheless, he was also beginning to realize that despite his talents and noble origins, he would never entirely fit in or be completely accepted by the French. Perhaps their manners and customs were too different from his own. Or perhaps Europeans in general were already becoming too familiar to him. Either way,

Pietro longed for something more, a life of adventure in some new, unexplored place.

He remembered the white spaces marked "unknown territory" on the map of Africa that he had seen years ago. Those blank spaces were fast disappearing. Pietro's preferred reading material had evolved from adventure novels to the travel diaries of real-life explorers, particularly those that spoke of Africa. He spent his spare time on the *Borda* absorbed by the writings of adventurers like Mungo Park, a Scotsman who had been among the first to explore West Africa; John Speke, who had traced the source of the Nile to Lake Victoria; and Richard Burton, the charismatic leader and brilliant linguist who was making his way through central Africa, later going on to Arabia and the Middle East. Pietro was especially fascinated by David Livingstone, a Scottish missionary who had been exploring and evangelizing Africa since 1849. Unlike the other explorers, Livingstone seemed to feel a genuine love and respect for the Africans, and wanted to give something back to the continent in exchange for all the personal and spiritual maturity it had given him. Livingstone was a fierce opponent of slavery, which he saw as one of the major plagues of Africa. At 17, Pietro was not and never would be a religious person, but he was a highly moral one, and he felt as Livingstone did. Pietro saw the enslavement of human beings as the contradiction of everything he stood for.

Slavery had been illegal in French territory since 1848, but beyond her national borders, France had little control over the still-thriving commercial phenomenon that benefited so many European traders, New World colonists, and African chieftains. France's navy patrolled the waters off the coast of her West African colonies in Senegal and Gabon, and apprehended slave ships from time to time, liberating the slaves and arresting the profiteers. As for what went on in the heart of Africa, beyond the trading posts and slave ports, that remained a mystery to Europeans. Every now and then a hardy explorer like Paul du Chaillu or Alfred Marche, a naval commander like Antoine Aymès, or a trader like the Englishman Bruce Walker would attempt to journey inland on one of the west African rivers, with limited success. The white men would sometimes establish treaties or a trading relationship with the inland tribes. Pietro read every detail of their reports as soon as they were published, but many of the young cadet's questions remained unanswered. Was there a navigable route into equatorial Africa? Where was the source of the great Congo River? Some of the accounts Pietro read seemed to contradict each other. Perhaps one day he would lead his own expedition, and find out the answers for himself.

In the early summer of 1870, Pietro graduated from the naval academy. He was justly proud of the achievement that had cost him so much effort, including four years of his youth spent in a foreign land, far from his family. Pietro's still-imperfect written French, as well as his choosing to concentrate his attention on the practical subjects he enjoyed most, gave him an average result: he graduated 44th in a class of 62 cadets. But most importantly, Pietro's years of training were over. Now he could look ahead to a life and career of his own, as a naval officer.

Pietro's graduation from the naval academy made 1870 a joyful year for him, but it would very soon become a catastrophic year for France. In July, Emperor Napoleon III, overconfident and unfamiliar with Europe's new realities, launched his nation into an ill-considered war with Prussia.

Only weeks later came a crushing defeat by a confederation of German states that no one had taken seriously. On September 2, the French army capitulated at the Battle of Sedan, and the Emperor himself was taken prisoner. The Prussians soon made their way to the outskirts of Paris and occupied the Château of St. Cloud, an imperial residence which rivaled Versailles in luxury and splendor. In October the Prussians pillaged the Château of St. Cloud and destroyed it with incendiary bombs fired from nearby Mount Valérien. France's humiliation now seemed total -- but it was only beginning.

The shocking series of defeats brought down the French government. Negotiations began with the Prussians, who demanded a war indemnity of five billion francs and the cession of the French provinces of Alsace and Lorraine. After bombardments and attacks on Paris, the Mayor surrendered the city, and France's Interim Government agreed to the terms of the armistice. The Parisians, however, refused to accept this humiliation. In March of 1871 they declared Paris an independent Commune and barricaded their city to keep the French and German armies from entering. France was now at war with its own capital city.

The Siege of Paris continued for two months, during which many Parisians were killed in the conflict or simply starved to death. In the bombardments, landmarks such as the Louvre and the City Hall suffered terrible damage. The Communards finally succumbed to the armies' advance in a bloody massacre at the end of May. This grisly civil war, and the loss of two of France's provinces, profoundly changed and demoralized French society. Now Germany seemed to dominate Europe, and it would take France many years to recover its lost national pride.

Pietro learned of these developments in the relative safehaven of Brest, where he awaited his first assignment as a naval officer. Faithful to his childhood dream, he had initially requested and obtained a place in the south Atlantic fleet patrolling the west coast of Africa, but the declaration of war had overruled the order. Now his Roman nationality made his participation in the Franco-Prussian conflict problematic. But after spending four of his formative years in Paris and Brest, Pietro felt a strong allegiance to France, and wanted to serve in the war against Prussia. Diligently making the rounds of his superiors at the naval academy and writing letters to the Ministry of the Navy in Paris to assure them of the sincerity of his vocation, Pietro managed to obtain an assignment on board the warship *Revenge*, embarking at Cherbourg for the North Sea. At 18, he was now a midshipman second class.

The sudden end of the war brought him back to Brest after only a few months. As he awaited his next assignment, Pietro thought about his future and was more certain than ever of his true calling. His most ardent desire was to spend his life as a French naval officer, be it in time of war or peace. Until now, Pietro's nationality had been determined by the political events around him. When he had left home to attend high school in Paris in 1866, Rome was not yet part of the Kingdom of Italy and still belonged to the Papal States. Pietro was therefore a Roman citizen like his father. In 1870, Italian troops entered Rome and the Papal States were annexed to Italy, with Rome as the Kingdom's capital. As a citizen of Papal Rome, a state which no longer existed, Pietro had to make a decision. With his parents' blessing, he requested French nationality in November of 1870. Although his status would not change officially until he reached the age of 21, Pietro had made his choice.

Early the following year he was assigned to another ship, the *Joan of Arc*, as part of naval force sent to quell the Kabyle insurrection in north Africa. While Kabylia was not the mysterious equatorial region that fascinated him most, it was Africa, nonetheless. Pietro was part of the landing force that was involved in bloody clashes with the Berber rebels near Bejaia, along the northern coast of present-day Algeria. These first combat experiences were sobering ones, as Pietro's idealized view of French rule and influence overseas came up against the reality of violent domination of a colonized people. Was this the only way? he wondered. Couldn't diplomacy, trade, or other incentives bring about some sort of cooperation to replace this senseless killing? Pietro kept these personal observations to himself, but they would not be forgotten.

Upon his return to Brest, Pietro passed the examination for the rank of midshipman first class. Hearing of a naval mission departing to patrol Africa's west coast, he was able to obtain an assignment on the frigate *Venus*. He was finally on his way to equatorial Africa, the land of his childhood dreams!

The main purpose of the *Venus*' two-year mission was to apprehend slave ships along the Gabonese coast. As had many others before him, Pietro realized that intercepting slave ships already on their way to the New World was much less effective than following the slave routes to their inland sources, and trying to combat the trade there. But penetrating the equatorial African interior still seemed impossible. The only known main waterway, the Congo, was blocked by rapids as it approached the Atlantic coast. There was another river, the Ogoway, but it was much narrower, and had yet to be explored.

As the *Venus* made its way south to the tropics, Pietro's imagination raced ahead of the ship, picturing the exotic lands that Livingstone and Aymès had described in their recent articles. On evenings when Admiral du Quillio and Commandant Duperré invited the junior officers to dine with them, Pietro plied his superiors with questions about the mysteries of African geography. What lay beyond the west African coast? Had they seen the Congo rapids? Was the Ogoway a tributary of another, larger river, or was it fed by a huge interior lake? Pietro's seemingly endless enthusiasm and curiosity on the subject earned him the jests of his shipmates. His friend Caradot drew a few cartoons of the would-be explorer's likely adventures in Africa. In one, Pietro was dressed as an amateur hunter with every weapon imaginable, coming up to a sign that said "Road Closed," while a tribe of cannibals behind him danced around a huge pot, surely expecting him to be their main course. In another cartoon, Pietro wore little more than a loincloth and was so emaciated that the cannibals had no use for him, and sent him on his way. Pietro laughed with the others, but his enthusiasm remained.

In July 1872, the *Venus* dropped anchor at the Gabon Estuary, and Pietro had his first sight of Libreville. For years he had dreamed of this fabled place that so many European explorers had described in their writings. A trading post had existed on the site since 1839, when a French lieutenant had befriended King Denis, the local chieftain. Ten years later, when a French frigate captured a slave ship and freed all of its prisoners, the liberated slaves founded a village next to the post and named it Libreville, "the city of the free." Pietro discovered a very young city, made up of mud and branch huts and a few European-style buildings on the green hills that surrounded the mouth of the Gabon River. It was a small but busy port where missionaries, traders, and adventurers crossed paths with local fishermen and their families, against a background of dense equatorial forest that was the domain of a tribe called the Pahouins. To Pietro, Libreville was his first step into a new world, and the name of the town had a profound symbolic meaning for him. Libreville's history of peace and freedom, its joining of French and African interests, represented exactly what he wanted to achieve in his career as an explorer.

Having acclimated well to the tropical heat and humidity, Pietro, Caradot, and another young officer named Latour were given a few days' leave to take a trip inland. They took a canoe to a small village along the Ogoway River where they traded needles and other European manufactured items for native daggers, bows, and arrows. Pietro was fascinated by his first glimpse of African culture, and he longed to go further inland, but apart from a few reconnaissance missions, his duties kept him near the coast.

In May of 1874, shortly before the *Venus* was scheduled to return to France, Pietro met the distinguished French naturalist Alfred Marche, a member of the Marquis de Compiègne's private expedition to equatorial Africa. Marche and Compiègne had just spent a year exploring the Ogoway River for a distance of four hundred kilometers inland, past the Booué Falls and up to its tributary, the Ivindo. Marche had studied the flora and fauna along the Ogoway's banks and felt that the region was "very rich and fertile" and that its inhabitants were "industrious and peaceful." Nevertheless, Marche and Compiègne had had to cut short their exploration for various reasons including tropical fevers, the many inland swamps that made navigation difficult, and a recent hostile encounter with the warlike Ossyeba tribe.

Pietro's appetite for adventure was whetted. He wanted to explore this mysterious continent, not under another officer's command, but according to his own plan. This year, if all went well, he would be promoted to ensign, a commissioned officer qualified to lead a small mission. As he completed his tour of duty along the African coast, he wrote out a proposal for an official French exploration of the Ogoway, to be led by him with a modest expeditionary force. It would be a geographical survey, giving the French government an idea of the natural resources and the navigational possibilities the area had to offer.

When the *Venus* returned to France in the summer of 1874, two pieces of good news awaited Pietro. The first was that his friend and patron, the Admiral de Montaignac, had just become Minister of the Navy. This meant that Pietro's proposal for the Ogoway mission would quickly make its way through the military hierarchy, and that it stood a good chance of being accepted. The second bit of news was that Pietro had been granted French nationality. As of August 12, 1874, he was a French naval officer in full, and would now sign his name as "Pierre Savorgnan de Brazzà."

Promising as it all seemed, Pietro (as his friends continued to call him) was still a bit apprehensive as he approached the Ministry of the Navy, in Paris' stately Place de la Concorde. Just as he had always had an innate affinity for nature and the sea, he had a fundamental mistrust of government offices and bureaucrats. They always seemed to want the one bit of information or the one piece of paper he did not have. What surprises would be in store for him this time?

Admiral de Montaignac was, as always, glad to see Pietro. He found the Ogoway mission proposal very interesting, and sent it on with his approval. Everything seemed to be working out, and Pietro was optimistic. He went to another office to see about further details of his mission -- only to be told that he would not be allowed even to take part in an African expedition, let alone lead one. Why? Because he had attended the naval academy and earned the grades of midshipman and ensign as a *foreign* naval officer. Now that he had been granted French citizenship, his record was wiped clean, and those qualifications could not be transferred. He would have to earn them all over again as a *French* naval officer. In point of fact, he was now nothing but a French seaman!

Pietro was speechless. Never had he imagined that his new name and nationality would erase the past six years of hard work. To hide his embarrassment he hurried out of the office and headed down the first stairway he saw. He was in such a state of distraction that, after all those years of scurrying up masts and sailing through storms, he slipped and fell on the marble staircase, and broke his arm.

CHAPTER THREE -- THE ENSIGN

In the autumn of 1874, while French Seaman Brazzà recovered from his broken arm and shattered naval career, life in Paris had returned to normal. Three years after the violent events of the Commune, the barricades were gone and the French capital was prospering.

Beneath business as usual, however, lay a palpable cynicism and a vague desire for new horizons and a new outlook on life. Escapist literature was all the rage, and illustrated newspapers and magazines were full of tales of adventure in exotic places. The railroad had transformed the average Frenchman's idea of traveling from a time-consuming and dangerous ordeal into an enjoyable leisure activity, and by now short trips, or at least a pleasant day in the country, were within everyone's reach.

Among the train travelers were a group of young artists who had lost patience with the restrictive methods taught at Paris' Academy of Fine Arts. They had begun a radical new technique of painting outdoors, not in the studio. Monet, Renoir, Pissarro, and others were experiencing nature firsthand, and inventing a new way to convey their visions of it. Art critics derisively called their works "impressionist" after Monet's "Impression: Sunrise." These young painters and their contemporaries, including the Parisian sculptor Auguste Rodin, were making the 1870s a decade of originality and personal expression.

Brazzà would need some originality to get him out of his current predicament. Fortunately, the physical recovery period for his broken arm gave him some time to reorganize his thoughts. His primary concern was trying to find a way to regain his lost rank, without performing six more years of service.

Assuming he managed that, he would then have to find support for his proposed mission to Africa. Besides the subsidies granted by the navy, he could possibly obtain financial support from scientific organizations like the Paris Geographical Society and the rapidly expanding Museum of Natural History. Surely the topographic and scientific findings of his mission would interest them. Brazzà's cousin, the Duchess Fitz-James, was very well-connected, and she could probably introduce him to many of Paris' important people. Lastly, how did one go about organizing an African expedition? Brazzà did not know a thing about the practical details. He would have to look into that as well.

He made many trips to the Ministry of the Navy, presenting his case to any officer who would listen. Even though his friend the Admiral de Montaignac was now Minister of the Navy, procedure had to be followed, and there seemed no way around the problem of his new nationality. Brazzà patiently explained again and again that even though he had attended the naval academy and served on French vessels under a different status from the one he now had, the fact remained that he still possessed the knowledge and experience he had earned during those years.

1. Brazzà as an Ensign in the French Navy, about 1875, aged 23. Photograph courtesy of the Bibliothèque Nationale de France, Paris.

He was convinced that he had every quality necessary to serve as an ensign in the French navy. All he asked was an opportunity to prove it.

By January of 1875, his many weeks of effort seemed to be getting him somewhere. He would be allowed to take a series of examinations, and would be given the rank corresponding to his result. Brazzà did his best, and in February he was awarded the rank of auxiliary ensign in the French navy.

At last he was a commissioned officer, qualified to take command of his first ship! A few weeks later, he was thrilled to learn that the Ogoway mission had been approved.

Over the course of the winter, the handsome 23-year-old count of Brazzà had become a regular at the Parisian aristocracy's social events, and he had made many useful contacts. Politicians like Léon Gambetta and Jules Ferry were taking an interest in his African mission. They saw it as a potential asset to the great colonial empire with which they hoped to restore France's former glory, and to rival the international prestige of Britain and Germany.

Scientists at the Museum of Natural History shared Brazzà's enthusiasm for the possible discovery of new species of plants and animals in the mysterious equatorial regions. Members of the Paris Geographical Society invited him to their informal Friday night dinners at the humble *Petite Vache* restaurant on the Left Bank -- a heartfelt gesture that turned out to be the most valuable favor of all.

Located in the midst of the Latin Quarter's venerable institutions, between the Sorbonne, the French Academy, and the Geographical Society, the *Petite Vache* (or "Little Cow") was nothing more than a dairy store with a small dining room at the back. Students had gotten into the habit of eating there, drawn by the simple yet delicious meals prepared by the dairyman's wife. Over the years a group of geographers and explorers had begun meeting in the back room every Friday night to share news and discuss past and future expeditions. Since the *Petite Vache* was not even a proper restaurant, the men could dine there in informal attire and could talk and smoke to their hearts' content.

One of the major topics of conversation at these Friday night gatherings was the recent passing of the great Scottish explorer, Livingstone, in the East African region he had loved so well. Livingstone's writings had been an inspiration to many in the group, and particularly to Brazzà. A few years earlier, when Livingstone seemed to have disappeared without a trace, he had been located by the Anglo-American journalist, Henry Morton Stanley. Apparently Stanley had now become an explorer in his own right, and was attempting to continue Livingstone's explorations, though certainly not his missionary work. While he shared Livingstone's courage and energy, Stanley was gaining a reputation as a brutal and intolerant commander. Amply financed by several wealthy American and British newspapers, Stanley's missions were well-equipped, well-staffed, and generally quite successful.

Brazzà, one of the youngest members of the *Petite Vache* group, spoke enthusiastically about his upcoming mission to the Ogoway. He had all sorts of questions for the more experienced explorers, and he noted their advice carefully. Over the course of many Friday nights and numerous follow-up meetings, Brazzà outlined everything he would need to do to make his mission a success.

2. An informal dining room at the back of a dairy shop, *la Petite Vache* was the convivial Friday-night meeting place of explorers when in Paris. This undated sketch is facetiously titled "A Meeting of the Academy of the *Petite Vache*" in reference to the prestigious French Academy located nearby. Drawing courtesy of the Bibliothèque Nationale de France, Paris.

His first task was obtaining subsidies to hire a staff and purchase all the supplies he needed. In approving his mission, the French navy had agreed to advance him a year's salary and provide him with a medical assistant and a quartermaster, as well as a dozen Senegalese marines and some Gabonese interpreters. They would also furnish scientific instruments and a basic supply of weapons to insure the men's safety. Brazzà's recently-made political contacts, Gambetta and Ferry, helped him obtain additional financial support from the Foreign Affairs and Education Ministries. The Paris Geographical Society followed suit with a modest subsidy. Brazzà completed his projected budget with a gift from his ever-supportive family in Italy. Many of Brazzà's new acquaintances were impressed with the single-minded efforts of this attractive young nobleman, who was willing to forego the comfortable life of an officer in Europe for the hardships and mysteries of a faraway land that had fascinated him since childhood.

Now that he had a budget, Brazzà's next concern was his staff. He had originally wanted to be the only European in the expedition, but he soon realized that at least one other representative of the French navy would be needed to take command if he became incapacitated. Victor Hamon had served with Brazzà on the *Venus*' two-year mission to Gabon, and Brazzà knew him to be a dependable, brave man, used to life along the African coast. Hamon would be the Ogoway mission's quartermaster, responsible for the transport and distribution of supplies.

With the help of the Museum of Natural History, Brazzà convinced the French government to authorize a naturalist to take part in the mission to collect samples of the minerals and the plant, animal, and bird life to be found in the little-known Ogoway region. This position would be filled by Alfred Marche, whom Brazzà had met the previous year in Gabon. Besides all his scientific expertise, the 31-year-old Marche was one of very few Europeans who had any practical knowledge of the Ogoway, making him an invaluable asset to the mission.

Parisian newspapers reported on the progress of Ensign Brazzà's plans, saying that he had hired most of his staff, and that the only remaining position to be filled was that of a young doctor to accompany the expedition. The newspaper notice caught the eye of Noël Ballay, a medical student at the University of Paris. He had recently finished his coursework and was planning a doctoral thesis on tropical diseases. Certainly some real-life experience in Africa would provide him with all the research data he needed. Making inquiries, the 28-year-old Ballay was invited to meet Brazzà at the next Friday night dinner at the *Petite Vache*. The meeting went well. Brazzà was impressed with Ballay's enthusiasm and sincerity, and hired him immediately. Now the nucleus of the mission was complete. The Senegalese marines and the Gabonese interpreters would be engaged in Africa.

The ensign's last major concern before leaving France was assembling all the equipment and provisions the mission would require. He had devoted much thought to the matter, and it was here that the originality of his philosophy and principles began to shine through. Brazzà was planning a new kind of mission of exploration with a new type of equipment: instead of the usual arsenal of guns and explosives, he ordered only a minimum of arms, and several tons of cloth, glassware and tools to be used for barter and as gifts for the tribal chieftains. He also purchased a huge quantity of fireworks for celebrations.

The young officer explained to his doubting superiors at the Ministry of the Navy that he wanted to learn as much as possible about the African tribes and their cultures. He intended to use violence only as a last resort, and to see how far diplomacy would take him. Needless to say, Brazzà's views met with a mixed reaction at the Ministry, but since he had been placed in charge of the Ogoway mission, decisions like these were his to make.

On the practical level, Brazzà was required to purchase French merchandise, normally from the Navy's usual suppliers in Rouen. He soon realized that he was going over budget, and at the last minute he managed to procure two additional subsidies from the Ministries of Commerce and Agriculture. Once the enormous amounts of foodstuffs, trade goods, scientific instruments, clothing, shoes, medicines, weapons, and everything else had been purchased, they were transported south to the naval base at Toulon, where Brazzà himself kept an eye on the shipment's progress. The goods were packed in double wooden crates, then encased in tin to prevent water damage.

Confiding the last details and preparations to Noël Ballay, Brazzà decided to leave for Africa in advance of his staff and supplies. The Ogoway mission had been assigned twelve Senegalese marines, reputed for their toughness and used to serving under French naval officers, to be hired by French officials in Dakar, and Brazzà wanted to participate in their training. He would embark on the naval transport *Pioneer*, departing from Bordeaux in late August. Even before he left France, Brazzà had already become something of a public figure, since reports of the young nobleman's upcoming African mission had been in the newspapers for months. He agreed to address the Geographical Society of Bordeaux on the eve of his departure.

On August 20, 1875, a cheering crowd lined the quais of Bordeaux. They bade good luck to the young man bound for a land whose destiny he would join to that of France, his adopted country, for at least a century to come.

CHAPTER FOUR -- THE FATHER OF SLAVES

After years of effort and months of minute preparations, the dream of Brazzà's young lifetime was becoming a reality. At 23, he was setting off to lead his own expedition into the heart of Africa. Confident and excited, he looked forward to six months or, if all went well, a year or more exploring new and uncharted territory that few white men had ever seen.

His superiors at the Ministry of the Navy, of course, expected little. After all, many older and more experienced explorers had failed in their attempts to penetrate equatorial Africa. A desultory survey of the coast, a report or two wired back from the trading posts at Libreville or Lambarene, a few forays into the bush before tropical illness or hostile tribes put an end to the would-be explorer's enthusiasm -- that was what these missions to Africa yielded, and young Brazzà's would be no different. Ministry officials had granted him funds for a stay of six months in Africa, but they doubted that the young nobleman would survive even that long before hastening back to civilization.

As the naval transport *Pioneer* weighed anchor at Bordeaux, then sailed past Portugal and Morocco on its way toward the equator, Brazzà had time to reflect on the challenges and adventures before him, the mysteries of Africa and its people, the cynicism of the French bureaucrats, the encouragement of the explorers at the *Petite Vache,* and the loving confidence in him that his mother had often expressed in her affectionate letters from Rome. Above all he remembered the words of the Scotsman whose life had helped to inspire Brazzà's dreams of exploration. Livingstone had written, "If a man goes with a good-natured, civil tongue, he may pass through the worst people in Africa unharmed."

Two weeks later Brazzà arrived at Saint-Louis du Senegal, a thriving colonial seaport and the hub of French commerce in West Africa. Meeting with officers at the French garrison, he was not entirely surprised to learn that no preparations whatsoever had been made for his mission. He set to work selecting a dozen Senegalese marines, who were duly sworn in. Since they were Muslim, they vowed their fidelity to France on the Koran. Brazzà began training them in the skills necessary for his expedition, including the handling of the new, lightweight Gras rifle, not yet a standard weapon in the French forces. The marines also received a few days' training in "how to march with shoes," an idea they accepted rather unwillingly. In fact, they quoted an African proverb stating that a person who wore shoes had something to hide, and could not be trusted. Fascinated by the lucidity and exuberance of African philosophy, Brazzà good-humoredly took note of the detail.

By late September the marines were ready, and Ballay, Marche, and Hamon had arrived in Saint-Louis with the supplies. Now virtually complete, the Brazzà mission set sail for Gabon.

They arrived in Libreville in late October, at the height of the autumn rainy season. Climatic conditions in equatorial Africa were at their most challenging, as the weather alternated between implacable sun and floods of rain. Brazzà found the administrative conditions equally challenging. In Libreville as in Saint-Louis, nearly nothing had been prepared for his mission. He had ordered five pirogues, the sturdy African dugout canoes used to navigate interior waterways, but only two had been purchased. When Brazzà tried to hire more, he found them much more expensive than anticipated. Speaking to traders, he learned that prices had been raised in the wake of the free-spending Dr. Oskar Lenz, a wealthy Austrian explorer who had recently passed through Libreville. Lenz was determined to be the first European to explore the equatorial rapids and the interior, and he had purposely paid fabulous prices for the supplies he needed, partly to create a good reputation for himself, but mostly to slow the progress of the rumored French expedition. Brazzà had heard that there was fierce competition among European explorers in Africa, but he hadn't expected to encounter it so soon. The only pirogues he found available were too heavy to navigate the rapids, but they would have to do. If competition was what Lenz wanted, then it was what he would get. Brazzà decided that he would catch up with Lenz before six weeks were out.

Unfortunately there was another problem more serious than weather or finances, and that was illness. Two of the marines fell ill with fever and had to be sent back to Senegal before the mission even began. The Europeans had difficulty acclimating to the tropical climate. Just as the cynical bureaucrats in Paris had warned him, things were not going as planned, but Brazzà was not discouraged. Instead of hiring two Gabonese interpreters, he engaged four, who would also help with cooking and would carry the hunting rifles.

On November 3, Brazzà, his men, and all their merchandise boarded the river steamer *Marabout* and set off for the settlement of Ilimba Rene, called Lambarene by the French, about 100 miles up the Ogoway River from the coast. The *Marabout* crossed the Gabon Estuary and headed down the Atlantic coast, then into the marshes of the lower Ogoway and along the river into the dense equatorial forest. During the steamer's slow progress, Brazzà and his companions gazed at the cathedral of greenery surrounding them: gigantic trees, hanging vines, tall grasses and water plants they had never seen before. Dazzled by the beauty, they also felt drugged by the intense heat and oppressive humidity. The air seemed to grow heavier and steamier the farther they sailed into the teeming forest.

After a few days they reached Lambarene, a trading post where British and other European companies had their agents. Brazzà and his staff disembarked and prepared to set up camp for a while, unloading their enormous quantity of supplies to take stock of what they had and what they would need for their progress up-river. The young commander was learning for himself that, just as the experienced travelers at the *Petite Vache* restaurant had told him, an expedition's greatest advantage and greatest liability lay in its baggage. In a barter economy, all goods and services had to be paid for with European fabrics, tools, and weapons. To hire porters, rowers, and pirogues to transport the supplies, one had to barter, and to barter, one needed more supplies, thus more to transport in the first place. Not only was Brazzà obliged to bring along all the food, clothing, shoes, medicine, and tools his men would need for a stay of at least six months in Africa, he had also had to pack a huge quantity of goods to exchange for transport or for any other services he imagined they might need. Not to speak of damage or pilferage, some amount of which was unavoidable on such a trip into the unknown. At the beginning of their adventure, the 156 crates of merchandise the mission carried, weighing a total of eight tons, seemed overwhelming.

Since they had left Libreville with only a couple of heavy pirogues, Brazzà's men needed to hire a few lighter ones and engage a number of rowers before they could go on any further. But as in many traditional societies, no business could be done in equatorial Africa before the tribal chieftain had had time to observe the foreigners, understand what it was they intended to do in his territory, and give them his stamp of approval. Gaining the favor of a local potentate was a slow process that took days, weeks, or even months of discussion, if it was successful at all. It was precisely at this juncture that most European expeditions began to encounter problems. In their home countries, business was a simple affair. They wanted something; they had the means to pay for it; they wished the transaction to be made as soon as possible, and that was that. Explorers were usually young, healthy, and quite inexperienced when it came to understanding cultures different from their own.

In this area as in so many others, Brazzà was different. His principal strengths were an inquiring mind, a sincere and equitable character, substantial personal charm, and inborn leadership qualities, but his background and early life had intensified these gifts. Brazzà's Mediterranean origins gave him a distinct advantage over the majority of French and British colonial officers, as he had been raised in Italy, a land where interpersonal skills are a highly developed art. At 23, he had already made the transition from a noble Italian upbringing to the spartan life of a French naval officer, and he had had the humbling experience of total immersion in a foreign language. His two nationalities reflected the northern and southern cultures he carried within him, and his achievements had given him a model of adaptation to other lifestyles that he took to heart. For the rest of his life, Brazzà would show great openness and respect toward foreign peoples and their customs.

Lambarene was located in the territory of the Inenga tribe. Their king, Renoke, had signed a treaty with the French ten years earlier, and was in theory under a French protectorate. In reality, little had changed since the arrival of the first white traders. No European went beyond Lambarene until Renoke had personally accepted him as his guest. Brazzà, a newcomer and leader of other white men, would have to be evaluated carefully. King Renoke prided himself on his good judgement and his profound knowledge of the human soul. As a young man, he had been told by a shaman that his intuition, or "inner sight," would be enhanced by the sacrifice of his "outer sight." Without hesitation, Renoke had blinded himself with scalding water. In his kingdom of magic and mystery, it was a small price to pay for supernatural powers.

Brazzà was led to the King's tent, where he presented the chieftain with gifts of fine fabrics. Speaking through interpreters, the two men conversed for hours. Brazzà was intrigued by the old man, who in turn came to know the explorer by the tone of his voice and by his reactions. As he observed Renoke's authority and dignity, and heard the story of his blindness, Brazzà sensed that he was on the threshold of a new and mystical world. He watched the King's gestures and tried to understand the unfamiliar words of the Inenga dialect. At the end of the interview, Brazzà returned to his camp, lost in thoughtful fascination at the sights and sounds of his first diplomatic encounter.

The days passed. Naturalist Alfred Marche, the only European member of the mission who had any experience in the African bush, went on ahead to the next village, checking on the availability and prices of boats, rowers, and porters. Brazzà, the quartermaster Victor Hamon, and the young doctor Noël Ballay stayed in their makeshift camp in Lambarene, writing letters and getting used to the heavy, soaking daily rains. Despite their constant fatigue, the men slept fitfully, sometimes in their uncomfortable camp beds, sometimes in hammocks slung between the enormous trees, trying to avoid the clouds of mosquitos, the armies of giant red ants, and the seemingly endless variety of monstrous insects. At first Brazzà, Hamon, and Ballay had little contact with the tribesmen, who regarded them warily and mistrustfully. The Inengas had become accustomed to white traders, but these Frenchmen seemed to want something else, and no one was quite sure what it was.

Every evening the tribe gathered around a fire for music and dancing that went on late into the night. Brazzà wandered over to see what was going on. Falling under the spell of the drumming and chanting and the agile, rhythmic movements of the brightly-painted dancers, he felt as if he had entered one of the adventure stories that had so engrossed him as a boy. Night after night he came to watch these extraordinary spectacles, and as time passed, he began to understand the symbolism and intricate meanings of each gesture, talisman, and sound.

Slowly the words of the Inenga language began to have meaning for him, and after a few weeks he could ask for food and play games with the children. For their part, the Inengas began to like this white man who spoke softly and chose to sit with them and share their meals. Meanwhile the parleys with Renoke continued. Every few days the King would send someone to bring Brazzà to him, and at each audience Brazzà offered more gifts, hoping that this would be the day Renoke would grant his approval for them to head off along the Ogoway to pursue their mission. But weeks passed without any mention of the approval. His conversations with Renoke began to seem aimless and repetitive. Brazzà felt his frustration mounting, but he tried to control his feelings. He sensed that time had a different meaning in Africa, and that this delay was another of Renoke's tests to determine the white leader's true character.

Obviously, if Brazzà's frustration had led to the use of force, he and his Senegalese marines could have subdued the Inengas in days, and proceeded wherever they liked, but that would have earned them the eternal hatred of this tribe and possibly many others. Like Livingstone before him, Brazzà was a man of peace, and he firmly believed that his greatest asset in this African undertaking would be the friendship of the tribesmen, no matter how long it took to obtain. As King Renoke and his honored white guest sat back and smoked more of Brazzà's precious European tobacco, the young French officer pondered his next move.

A constant of life in the forest was the continual quarrelling between neighboring tribes. As have so many outsiders before and since, Brazzà saw this intertribal strife as the means to accomplish his ends. Alfred Marche returned from the next village up-river to report that the prices the neighboring tribe, the Bakalais, demanded for the hire of pirogues, rowers, and porters were nearly as exorbitant as what the Inengas were asking. Brazzà shrewdly instructed Marche to return to the Bakalais, agreeing to their prices for the hire of all the supplies and staff they required. No sooner was this done than word of the deal came back to the Inengas, who were mortified at the loss of this business in favor of their despised neighbors. By this time Brazzà had spent two months as a guest of the Inengas, and even King Renoke was beginning to realize that he could not retain the white man forever, much as he appreciated Brazzà's tobacco and gifts. He had sensed Brazzà's determination, and he knew that the young commander would eventually carry out his plans in Africa. Better to get as much out of him as quickly as possible, before the white man lost patience and began trading with other tribes.

The official pronouncement was made: Renoke granted Brazzà his friendship and approval, and agreed to sell him 9 large pirogues and rent him 100 rowers for the most reasonable price yet. French axes, rifles, gunpowder, copper wire, mirrors, salt, and tobacco were handed over to the Inengas, and the deal was accomplished. Brazzà had passed his first test in Africa.

At the same time as this practical achievement, Brazzà's humanitarian ideals were coming up against the hard realities of life in the forest. Slavery, illegal in French territory since 1848, was still alive and well throughout Africa, and Brazzà knew that Renoke would probably use his newly-acquired supplies to trade for more slaves, who would then be resold on the coast to the Portuguese. Brazzà could only hope that the slaves would be apprehended and freed by patrolling French troops, as was often the case. Another matter was the choice of trade goods. Fabrics and manufactured items had their value, but the tribesmen kept asking for something else.

"All they want is 'alugu' – brandy – that's all I hear!" complained Brazzà to Ballay. "And to think I brought only a minimal amount of alcohol, for humanitarian reasons! But we have to be realistic. I'm putting my humanitarian ideas aside for now. I've ordered 400 liters of brandy from the coast."

After two months in Lambarene, the mission readied itself for passage to their next destination, the smaller trading post of Lope, another hundred miles upstream. Beyond Lambarene, the Ogoway was too narrow to accommodate steamers, and so everything had to be loaded onto pirogues. On January 13, 1876, a few weeks before his 24th birthday, Brazzà set off at the head of an impressive fleet of a dozen pirogues, each one 50 feet long and 3 feet wide, propelled by up to 20 rowers. The boats were packed with merchandise, and Brazzà sat immobile on a crate, unable to move without upsetting the carefully-balanced pile. Tall and thin, with his dark hair and dark eyes and the white turban he sometimes wore to shield him from the sun, Brazzà would be remembered by some of his colleagues as looking like an Arab prince.

Heading northeast against the current, Brazzà and his more than a hundred men developed a daily routine, doing their best to withstand the stifling heat and the daily floods of rain. "We leave at dawn and go until noon," Brazzà noted. "Then we stop on a sand bank and have lunch. At two in the afternoon we get going again until about five. Then onto another sandbank where we prepare to spend the night, trying to get out of the rain as best we can, not an easy task." Besides the heat of the day, the rowers had to contend with other dangers, like the clouds of bees who occasionally settled on them, forcing them to jump into the river to escape the burning pain of the stings. When preparing meals, the cooks put clay into the fire to produce smoke, keeping insects away from the food as it cooked. Everyone ate under mosquito netting. The only source of drinking water was the river, even though it sometimes had animal carcasses floating in it. And as for a good night's sleep, "the nightly rains have us all swimming around in mud, no matter how we try to cover or insulate ourselves," Brazzà wrote.

Despite all the hardships, Brazzà proved himself to be an able commander. He was quiet and attentive while his men chatted, expansive and enthusiastic when he spoke about his plans. He was generous and shared everything he had, but he sometimes showed his temper if not obeyed. By turns polite and charming, he was also crafty, and tested his men by pretending to sleep so he could hear their quarrels and complaints, and at times left objects of value in plain sight to draw out a thief. The young nobleman took his role as leader of the expedition very seriously.

On January 16th, they arrived at the village of Samkita. Noël Ballay was very ill with malaria and could go no further, so for several days Brazzà tended the doctor as best he could. The commander himself had never had malaria, but he knew that it was only a matter of time. No European who traveled in equatorial Africa was spared the painful, exhausting ordeal of fever, vomiting, and dysentery -- and unfortunately, 19th- century medicines like laudanum and quinine used to treat malaria were ordeals in themselves. Many travelers never recovered, or if they did, decided to turn back while they still had the strength to return home. Brazzà prayed that poor

Ballay, delirious and unable to eat, would not only regain his health, but manage to maintain his faith in the expedition.

Proceeding without their doctor was risky. There could be a serious accident or illness, not to mention the infected blisters and injuries the porters and rowers incurred every day, but Brazzà didn't want to lose any more time. He decided to leave Ballay in Samkita in the care of Victor Hamon, and resume the journey with some of the marines. Trailblazer Alfred Marche was already heading for Lope, and Brazzà set off to join him, guided by the escort that King Renoke had assigned him.

At this point the Ogoway narrowed even further, and the rapids began. Brazzà and his fleet of pirogues made a good start, rowing against the current, conquering the rapids, and making some hard-won progress upstream, though they were often terrified by the brute force of the rushing river. After a few days of this harrowing effort, they came to a hellish series of rapids that proved too much for them. Seven pirogues were overturned, many crates of merchandise were lost -- and a number of rowers sank below the surface and drowned. Making his way to the bank and counting the survivors, Brazzà scanned the river for any trace of the missing men -- *his* men, under *his* responsibility -- and saw nothing but the ruthless torrent. This mission of exploration, he realized sorrowfully, was proving expensive indeed.

They managed to salvage some of the sunken crates, but the food, clothing, and scientific instruments they contained were ruined. Saving what items they could and leaving them on the riverbank to dry, Brazzà and his men set up camp for the night. The next morning, they were back on the river. In the days that followed, they continued on as prudently as they could, taking refuge in the forest when a strong wind came up to blow the daily rains into a tornado. Eventually they came to the last Inenga village.

"What will become of us once we're out of Renoke's territory?" Brazzà asked the escort the King had given them.

"You will be in the land of the Okandas, and then of the Ossyebas."

"Have they seen white people?"

"They've traded with them. But they don't like them entering their territory."

Brazzà had heard stories of European skirmishes with these tribes. Alfred Marche, who did not share Brazzà's deep reserve of patience, had had a hostile encounter a few years earlier. When a chief had threatened him with a weapon, Marche had immediately ordered his men to tie up the chief, and he demanded that the tribesmen make reparation by presenting him with one of their animals before their leader was released. They complied, but in anger Marche had the animal killed, dismembered, and thrown into the river to show his contempt. A short time later, several of Marche's pirogues had disappeared.

Brazzà had some long conversations with his escort in an attempt to learn as much as he could about the Okanda and Ossyeba tribes so that he would know what to expect. As Brazzà approached each village, said the guide, there would be a show of weapons and aggressive demeanor. This did not mean that the tribe was actually hostile. It was intended simply to give the visitors an idea of the tribe's strength and the high price they would have to pay to pass through unharmed. After this symbolic display, Brazzà could arrange a peaceful meeting with the tribal chieftain, making sure, of course, to offer valuable gifts. Thereafter things would go more or less as they had with Renoke. The chief would offer hospitality and try to keep the white man as long as possible, to obtain the maximum number of gifts. He would warn Brazzà of the dangers of the next tribe up the river. But the chieftain would not retain the visitor by force. It was mostly a contest of will and diplomacy. A chess game, thought Brazzà.

On February 10, 1876, Brazzà's expedition arrived at Lope, a tiny village that came to life every year at this time, when the Inengas and Okandas held their annual slave market. The young explorer, preferring not to witness scenes of an activity he considered reprehensible, had his men set up camp on a rise along the riverbank at a distance from the trading. They built a large shed for the mission's merchandise and set up their tents carefully, since the expedition would have to spend several months in Lope. The Ogoway was currently in its flood stage, and Brazzà's rowers refused to go any farther until the water level went down, probably in April. Several of the Senegalese marines and the Gabonese interpreters were ill, and Brazzà himself was beginning to feel feverish. Learning that the infamous Dr. Lenz was nearby, Brazzà immediately went to meet him, bringing him some mail from the coast and hoping to obtain medical assistance. Lenz received him very cordially, but disappointed him with the news that his doctorate was in geology, not medicine! The young ensign was, however, not surprised to learn that after all Lenz' generous spending, the doctor was now out of funds and would be returning to the coast. Brazzà mentioned that he would soon be sending a convoy back to Libreville, and invited the doctor to travel with them, for safety.

Returning to camp, Brazzà received a message from Ballay saying that his health was a little better and that he awaited further orders. Brazzà decided to send the sick marines and interpreters to Samkita to meet Ballay, who could escort them back to Libreville where they could all make a complete recovery, and where replacements could be hired, if necessary. Brazzà also sent an emissary asking Ballay to forward the rest of the merchandise on to him in Lope.

Realizing that he would not be leaving Lope for several months, Brazzà put his time to good use by making sketches and writing detailed descriptions of the local flora and fauna. By night, he observed the stars and planets and made calculations as he had learned to do in his celestial navigation classes at the naval academy. Seeing him use his sextant and other astronomical instruments, the tribesmen assumed he was communicating with the heavenly bodies, and Brazzà did nothing to discourage that impression. He knew that he was in a land where magic was considered a powerful, omnipresent force, and being thought of as some sort of wizard would certainly do him no harm when it came time to bargain with the chief.

As he had done with the Inengas, Brazzà paid a series of courtesy calls on the Okandan chieftain, offering him gifts. The explorer took part in the meals and activities of the tribe, studying their ways and noting his observations in his journal. When he decided it was time to make an especially good impression, he set off some of the fireworks he had brought along, and gave the Okandas an unforgettable show. Much as the French bureaucrats had derided him for spending part of his supply budget on fireworks, Brazzà had known they would make for an extraordinary event in equatorial Africa, and they did.

One night, as Brazzà slept in his camp bed beneath the mosquito netting, he was startled awake by a piercing scream. He had barely disentangled himself when a runaway slave threw himself at Brazzà's feet, begging him for protection. The slave, a prisoner from one of the many intertribal conflicts, had broken his chains and was seeking help from "the great white man." In hot pursuit of the fugitive was his Okandan owner, angrily demanding his "property" or an equivalent payment.

Brazzà took a few minutes to evaluate the situation. As a French officer, he was authorized to confiscate the slave and arrest his owner, but doing so would give serious offence to the Okandas, his hosts. That was unthinkable. Then again, he could hardly ignore the frantic slave's cries for help. His only option was to purchase the captive's freedom. Brazzà produced the astronomical sum of 400 French francs and offered it to the owner, who gladly accepted. The liberated prisoner pledged his loyalty to Brazzà over and over, promising that he would be the best slave the white man had ever had. Brazzà explained to him, through an interpreter, that he was now a free man, and could go home if he chose. If he stayed to work for Brazzà, then he would be paid, like the others.

News spread quickly that the white chief was mad enough to offer fabulous prices for slaves, only to free them and then to pay them more to work for him as rowers! No one had ever heard of such behavior. Soon enough, the French camp was surrounded by slaves begging for their freedom. Brazzà stared at all the expectant faces, and simply could not believe that his quick decision in the middle of the night had provoked such a phenomenon. But far from regretting his act, he was glad of it. As a young cadet he had dreamed of coming to Africa and freeing slaves, and here was his dream coming true! He had been sent to this continent as a naval officer of France, his adopted country, and was fully empowered to make these slaves free men. What better way to show that Europe had something valid and civilized to offer Africa, besides all the guns and the brandy?

All that was needed now was some way to give solemnity and meaning to this momentous occasion. Brazzà thought back to all the nights he had spent watching tribal dances and celebrations. He remembered the importance of gestures and stance, of traditional dress and symbolic objects. Searching through his baggage he produced a French flag, planted it in the ground, and announced, "This flag is the symbol of France. In our country, no man has the right to hold another man as a slave. Any slave who touches this flagpole will be free." Brazzà invited the slaves to come forward, one by one, to touch the staff. As each did so, the Senegalese marines broke the chains around his ankles. Lastly, Brazzà had both the newly freed slaves and the marines line up to salute the flag.

The Okandan tribesmen couldn't believe their eyes. For many years they had sold slaves, white men had bought them, and everybody had made money. But this white leader was different. Even if his actions were costing them some profits, they had to admire his bravery and his faithfulness to his principles. And though the Okandas made money from the slave trade, they, like all African tribes, lived in constant fear of being conquered and enslaved in their turn. True to his word, Brazzà gave the freed slaves the choice of leaving or working for him, and they all stayed, perhaps out of fear, or exhaustion, or pure curiosity. They learned the routine of the French camp and worked alongside the other porters and rowers. A few weeks later, Brazzà sent them out into the forest to gather food, and even gave them rifles to protect themselves! Even the slaves were stunned. But at the end of the day, every single one came back to camp. Brazzà had proven his point: free men do better work and are more loyal. Fairness had been shown to be more effective than force.

These months of "wasted time" had been put to good use after all. After six months in Africa, Brazzà had made little headway into unexplored territory, but he had taken a great stride in the esteem of the Africans. His good reputation among the tribes was fast becoming a legend. The young officer had earned another title to add to that of ensign: to the people he had freed, he was known as "the Father of Slaves."

Despite his moral achievement, as the weeks passed, Brazzà became restless and dissatisfied. His rowers still claimed the water was too high to take to the river, and Lope had little to offer him. "Since January 12," Brazzà wrote in April, "I haven't slept indoors or had a table to write on. The heat of the day gives way to freezing cold and wind at night. The fire burns your face without warming your body." He was losing patience with the Okandas, and began thinking about how to gain the favor of the next tribe, the Ossyebas, reputed to be aggressive and intractable because of their relative isolation and rare contact with whites. He sent them an emissary to propose a meeting, but they showed no interest. Brazzà needed a way to attract their attention and arouse their curiosity.

He knew that his Winchester repeating rifle, which could fire fourteen shots in succession, always made a strong impression on African tribesmen. At the same time every day, he began going to the border of Okanda and Ossyeba territory and, alone and apparently oblivious to his surroundings, he cleaned his rifle and engaged in some target practice. After an hour or so of that, he got out his sextant and held it up to the sky while he made many measurements. To the Ossyebas watching from the bush, he seemed to be conversing with the spirit world, and receiving magical tools and talents from them. The witnesses gave a detailed description of the mysterious actions of the "white shaman," as they were beginning to call him, to the Ossyeba chief Mamiaka, who became increasingly curious.

A few weeks later, Brazzà was invited to pay a visit to Mamiaka's court. The explorer was thrilled at the success of his stratagem, and he and a couple of his marines followed the escort through the territory of the fearsome Ossyebas on their way to meet the chief. Unlike the Okandas, whose lives revolved around river trade, the Ossyebas made a cult of war. Besides their menacing air, they filed their teeth to points, colored their beards a bright red, tattooed their skin, and wore necklaces made of human bones and panther teeth. At the sight of these exotic, magnificent apparitions, Brazzà again had the feeling that he had entered one of the adventure stories that he had so loved as a boy.

The meeting with Mamiaka went well. Brazzà made skillful use of both diplomacy and showmanship. "The Ossyebas were distant but hospitable," he noted in his journal. "After two days we had become friends. I showed them some rockets, long-range rifles, explosives, and what amazed them the most, some phosphorescent magnesium." Once he had been accepted by the Ossyebas, Brazzà's next step was to give his former hosts, the Okandas, the impression that he had new contacts and that he no longer needed them. He managed to convince Chief Mamiaka to pay a visit to the Okandas to prove the point. The visit took place, and both chiefs seemed impressed with the explorer, but both still hesitated to provide the large number of tribesman that Brazzà wanted to employ. His new hosts took him on some reconnaissance trips in the region, and introduced him to a few other chieftains, but Brazzà still felt frustrated by his painfully slow progress in equatorial Africa. It had now been eight months since his departure from France, two months past the initial six-month period allotted for his mission, and what had he accomplished? He had followed the Ogoway River for two hundred miles, and had progressed only slightly beyond the trading post of Lope, as had other whites before him. He had covered no new territory.

To force the issue, Brazzà planned a meeting with all the chiefs he had met thus far. Again he thought carefully about the symbolic actions and attitudes used by the tribes he had visited and studied, and about how he should speak and act. He had an important message to convey, and he would not be given a second chance.

Finally, the Inenga, Bakalai, Okanda, and Ossyeba chiefs, along with some of their allies, gathered for the parley with the white leader. Brazzà entered the meeting with a serious air, holding gifts in his left hand, his rifle in his right. "The white man has two hands," he told them. "One bears gifts, the other death. There is nothing in between. We will go up your river, either bringing trade which is profitable for you, or scorching the riverbanks with our powerful weapons. The choice is yours. Only you can decide if our passage will be a blessing or a curse for your peoples. Will our path be strewn with gifts? Or will the Ogoway run red with blood? You, the rulers of your tribes, will decide."

There was a moment of silence. Then Brazzà could see that his carefully thought-out plan had made an impression. He returned to his camp to await the chieftains' reply. The next day, one of the Ossyeba chiefs came to see him. Brazzà's way was open, he said. The chief's own son and fourteen brave warriors would escort the explorer more than a hundred miles along the Ogoway, to the land of the Adoumas, and would introduce him as a friend.

Brazzà thanked him and accepted his generous offer. Later that evening, relieved and gratified by the chiefs' decision, the young ensign reflected on his hard-won progress. Making his way down the river and through the equatorial forest with all his men and merchandise, difficult, dangerous, and excruciating as that was, still seemed easier than these endless negotiations. Many times in the future he would be glad of all he had learned from his extended stays with the tribes, and grateful for the enduring friendships he had forged, but for now he turned his attention to the road ahead. Calling his men together, Brazzà began organizing their departure into a wild, mysterious region where no white man had gone before.

CHAPTER FIVE -- THE BAREFOOT CONQUEROR

In May 1876, Brazzà prepared to leave Lopé on foot with a small party that included Denis, his reliable interpreter, Metoufa and Balla-Touré, two Senegalese marines, and a few porters. They were accompanied by Zabouré, nephew of the Ossyeba chief Mamiaka, and fourteen of his warriors. Zabouré would escort Brazzà overland for more than 100 miles due east, rejoining the Ogoway River at the Doumé Falls. There he would introduce Brazzà to the eastern Ossyeba and Adouma chiefs, who could help him make further progress. Meanwhile Victor Hamon and Alfred Marche would remain at the French camp in Lopé with the rest of the expedition and most of the baggage. Noël Ballay was still recuperating in Libreville.

Zabouré, Brazzà, and their followers started off on a fairly easy trail, then waded knee-deep down the course of a stream before entering the dense forest where the mud, vines, branches, and fallen tree trunks hindered their progress. Recent rains had made everything slippery. The thick canopy of trees protected the men from the heat of the sun, but there was so little light that they were obliged to keep track of the group by calling out to each other, their voices echoed softly by the cries of the forest animals. The day's journey ended earlier than it would have on the river, since by sunset they found themselves already plunged in darkness. Having covered only five miles, they prepared to spend their first night in the forest.

Much to the surprise of Brazzà and his men, in a short time Zabouré's warriors had deftly set up a comfortable, dry camp in the wet forest, and had begun cooking a supper of plantains. Brazzà slung his hammock between two trees, and hung a light blanket over a branch to form a tent.

Their next few weeks in the forest would not be so easy. The rainy season began in earnest, and they often had to spend entire days in wet clothes, scrambling on all fours between overgrown trees and vines, and crawling along huge, decaying trunks that formed the only bridges across the forest's rivers and streams. Zabouré's warriors had brought a limited supply of food, assuming that with his superior European rifles, Brazzà could easily hunt enough game to feed everyone. One way or another, he managed to do so.

Occasionally they would have the luxury of spending the night in a village. In these regions where Europeans were virtually unknown, Brazzà found himself even more of a public figure than he had been on the day of his departure from Bordeaux. His every move was observed and critiqued by a crowd of villagers. Some tribesmen, hearing that Brazzà was a brave man, would try to surprise him at unexpected moments with weapons or war cries, to see if the white man would show fear. Everyone watched carefully as he ate, and as he settled in for the night. Their interest seemed to reach its climax as he removed his shoes. Seeing his bare feet, they cried "He has five toes!" and, apparently satisfied, the villagers left him in peace until the next morning.

By mid-June, Zabouré had guided the small party to the vicinity of the Doumé Falls and introduced Brazzà to King Joomba, the local Ossyeba chieftain. Joomba had heard many stories about the "white shaman" and was anxious to impress Brazzà. The explorer and his men were received with a fine banquet, over which the King presided, surrounded by his wives and his friends' wives, whom he introduced as his own. The welcoming banquet coincided with the tribe's circumcision ceremony. Brazzà made use of the opportunity to learn about traditional practices and beliefs. He paid close attention to everything he saw, and noted it all in his journal.

The time had come to bid farewell to Zabouré and his warriors, to whom Brazzà gave gifts in gratitude for their unfailing guidance and protection. The explorer set up camp in Joomba's village while he planned the next leg of his journey. Joomba seemed delighted to offer his hospitality. He saw to the guests' needs and placed his and his friends' wives at their disposal. His own daughter, Malonga, served as Brazzà's private cook. Brazzà was satisfied with her cooking, but noted that she seemed a bit disappointed that they did not enter into a more intimate relationship. While he wrote out his letters and reports, she would come and sit near him and ask him to paint her face with the ink, or to write her name in his language on her chest as a sort of tattoo. She claimed to be very dissatisfied with the neighboring chiefs her father wanted her to marry. Eventually realizing that Brazzà's intentions toward her remained friendly but professional, she began turning her attention to Denis and the marines. To Malonga's father, of course, intermarriage with a "white chief" would have meant an unlimited supply of rifles, gunpowder, and other rare and valuable European merchandise.

After a week or so, Brazzà expressed a desire to continue his explorations, first making certain that the King would not see the guests' departure as an affront to his hospitality. Brazzà and Denis began with a short excursion on foot in the immediate area, to the Doumé Falls. The young ensign was the first European to see the waterfall, since it was located in what had been up to then considered "hostile territory" to explorers. Brazzà returned to Joomba's village to find Dr. Lenz, who still hadn't made up his mind to return to Europe. Despite their fierce professional rivalry, Brazzà and Lenz spent a few days chatting amicably about their experiences, and traveling in convoy to visit some of the nearby Adouma villages. But soon Lenz, exhausted and impoverished after two years in Gabon, decided to begin his trek back to Libreville where he finally left Africa, never to return.

For his part, Brazzà felt restless and dissatisfied with his slow progress. Although his meetings in the different villages seemed to go well, none of the Ossyebas or Adoumas ever produced the pirogues that they had agreed to sell him. Brazzà was convinced that Joomba and the other chieftains were toying with him. In July, he gave Joomba an ultimatum, saying that if the pirogues were not delivered in a few days, Brazzà and his men would leave the village. Joomba agreed to make good his promises, but then changed his mind again. Losing patience with these fruitless attempts at bargaining, Brazzà got into a heated argument with Joomba, during which Balla-Touré, one of the marines, laid hands on the King to restrain him. Joomba was furious that Brazzà had dared to have him handled so roughly by "a slave," and swore to have the spirits of his royal ancestors invoke a curse on the white man.

Denis, Brazzà's interpreter, warned the explorer to be careful. "Joomba will cast an evil spell on you. He is a powerful wizard."

"Nonsense!" replied Brazzà. On the contrary, he hoped that the unpleasant incident would somehow resolve the situation. That evening he was reassured to see one of Joomba's wives bringing him a large jar of pineapple wine. Brazzà drank it with pleasure, but only hours later he became violently ill with a high fever and uncontrollable vomiting. Denis and the entire village saw this as evidence of the ancestors' curse. Brazzà, delirious and nauseated, bitterly regretting his own trust and goodwill in accepting the wine, suspected poisoning.

For the next few days Brazzà was too feverish and weak to leave his hut or even to eat anything. Joomba guiltily consulted his shamans, and when they told him that the ancestral spirits gave no sign of Brazzà's eventual recovery, the King became anxious and fearful. What if Brazzà died in his village? And what if an army of powerful white men came to avenge his death? Immediately, one of the pirogues Brazzà had been expecting for so long was made ready, and four tribesmen were ordered to escort Brazzà anywhere he wanted to go, as soon as he became well enough to travel.

Although he was still in a weakened state, five or six days later Brazzà decided to take advantage of these unusual circumstances in order to leave the village and cover some new ground. But after a short time on the river, the rowers Joomba had assigned to him began asking insistently to go ashore. Brazzà realized that the scheme had been simply to get him out of Joomba's territory! The tribesmen were planning to abandon him here on the Ogoway, just before the rapids, with only his two men and a paltry amount of supplies! Joomba's men knew that Brazzà was too weak to pursue them, and if the white man died here, he was neither their guest nor their responsibility.

Brazzà ordered them to continue rowing. The tribesmen began to rock the pirogue violently, attempting to tip it over, to give them a chance to escape. Brazzà and Denis took out their rifles and ordered them to stop, on pain of death. The rocking continued, and Brazzà fired a shot that grazed the ear of one of the tribesmen. They rocked the boat even harder, and just as it seemed about to capsize, Brazzà and Denis each fired a shot at the same time. Two of the rowers, mortally wounded, fell backwards into the river, while the other two jumped and swam to shore. Managing to keep the small craft afloat, Brazzà let the fugitive rowers disappear into the forest.

Brazzà, Denis, and Balla-Touré were now alone in the pirogue, where they faced the prospect of getting through the unfamiliar rapids on their own. Brazzà, drained of his strength, lay flat in the bottom of the boat while Denis, at the prow, and Balla-Touré, at the stern, spent the next twelve hours maneuvering the pirogue through the torrent. At nightfall, they went ashore at a village where, drenched and exhausted, they slept right on the river bank.

Brazzà awoke to the sound of the rhythmic chanting of a convoy of Okandan rowers. A flotilla of 22 pirogues appeared, bearing Noël Ballay, Alfred Marche, and a large stock of supplies! Stunned and overjoyed, Brazzà and his men went to greet the comrades they hadn't seen for three long months. Hearing of the difficulties with Joomba and the terrible shooting incident on the river, Ballay and Marche explained that the Okandans were very possibly behind these problems. They had become resentful at not being Brazzà's only hosts, guides, and trading partners in the region, and had apparently convinced Joomba and his neighbors to prevent Brazzà's progress as long as they could. The Okandans still refused to let the French expedition leave their territory altogether, and had insisted that Victor Hamon remain in Lopé with the rest of the merchandise.

Ballay gave Brazzà a complete check-up and diagnosed fatigue due to malnutrition, and some lung congestion. He prescribed at least a week of complete rest for the young commander, but Brazzà, promising to lay absolutely still in the pirogue, prevailed upon the doctor to let him accompany the mission a little further down the Ogoway. The convoy traveled on to N'ghémé, where they planned to set up camp for a while. For the next few days Ballay noted that Brazzà's health was deteriorating alarmingly, and that he looked positively skeletal. As soon as they arrived at N'ghémé on August 24, 1876, Brazzà was immediately carried to a hut where he would agonize for more than a month.

Having abused his body nearly to the breaking point, the 24-year-old ensign was now barely able to move, and was too ill to take any nourishment but a little water boiled with sugar cane. The heat, the insects, a questionable water supply, the possible poisoning in Joomba's camp, combined with physical exhaustion and the constant stress of leading an expedition through some of the world's harshest terrain, had simply become too much for him. The shock of the river incident, where Brazzà and Denis had killed two tribesmen, had finally overwhelmed the little resistance he had left. Ballay was deeply concerned, and watched carefully over his patient. The young doctor sent word to the neighboring Adouma chiefs that his commander was gravely ill. He did so partly to request their help and support, and partly to show them the result of the delaying tactics and temper tantrums that had proved to be so frustrating and dangerous. The chiefs, many of whom genuinely liked Brazzà, offered food and traditional medicines, and promised to be more cooperative with the travelers.

Every day, two N'ghémé villagers moved Brazzà and his bamboo cot to the outside of his hut, where he spent the daylight hours resting in the shade of a huge tree that spread its branches over the river. He gazed at the fertile hills that surrounded the village, and at fields planted with manioc, pistachios, and palm and banana trees. He watched the rituals of everyday life in the village: the fishermen on the nearby bank, the hunters returning with guinea fowl, the village women tending crops or preparing meals. He was entertained by the chief's children, who had been sent to keep him company, and by a constant stream of curious villagers. As he gradually improved, he was able to drink milk with honey. By October, his strength had returned.

During Brazzà's convalescence, Marche had reconnoitered the next 60 miles of the Ogoway. Apart from a few patches of rapids, it was navigable up to the confluence with its large tributary, the M'passa, which could in turn lead to one of the great African lakes, or perhaps to an even larger river. Brazzà was anxious to follow this promising itinerary and to solve the mystery of the central African rivers and their sources, but before the mission went any further, they had to retrieve Victor Hamon and the rest of the party and supplies that were still being held by the Okandas. It was decided that Brazzà himself would return to Lopé to resolve this problem. While he was gone, Ballay would assume command of the camp in N'ghéme, and recuperate from his efforts of the past few months during Brazzà's illness. Marche would spend the time gathering samples and making notes of the local flora and fauna for Paris' Museum of Natural History.

On October 27, 1876, Brazzà set off, heading back down the Ogoway toward Lopé with a group of the Okandan rowers. Much to his dismay, the rowers and their chief had purchased 180 slaves whom they were transporting back to their Okandan village for forced labor or eventual re-sale. Brazzà was not pleased with the situation, but under the circumstances, there was little he could do. As the convoy made a brief stop at Joomba's village, Brazzà was invited to meet with the contrite King, who entreated the explorer to forget the bitter arguments they had had, and to regard him as a friend. Brazzà was glad to do so.

Brazzà and the Okandans continued down the Ogoway, making their way through the deadly rapids. One of the Okandan pirogues capsized, and a number of the slaves, helpless in their wooden shackles, struggled frantically in the torrent. Jumping into the river, Brazzà managed to save a few of the slaves, but despite his urging, the Okandas watched fatalistically and passively as several others drowned.

The next day, the convoy arrived in Lopé. This little town that nine months earlier had looked to Brazzà like nothing more than a dingy group of shacks in the middle of nowhere, now seemed to offer all the comforts of home. The villagers welcomed the young explorer warmly. Brazzà greeted Victor Hamon and the Senegalese marine Metoufa before taking up residence in the simple house he had helped build the previous spring. It was a cabin made of bamboo, with a veranda where Brazzà liked to sit in his improvised easy chair. The journey from N'ghémé had again exhausted him, and the dampness of the drenching trip through the rapids had brought back the congestion in his lungs. He would need to spend several months recuperating in Lopé.

The news of his arrival spread rapidly, and Brazzà's many acquaintances in the region came to pay him a call. The Inenga chief Renoke was among them. Brazzà was touched by the many visits he received, and although many were motivated by simple curiosity, the explorer felt that he was developing real friendships in this town. Of course, he was still treated as something of a curiosity. Villagers brought their children to see the unusual sight of a white man, and new mothers came to show him their babies, asking Brazzà to hold or touch the child. According to local superstition, this would bring the baby good luck.

Between visits, Brazzà sat on the veranda admiring the dramatic beauty of the landscape. The Okanda country was dominated by grassy plains, encircled by the majestic Okeko mountains. Lopé's strategic location on the Ogoway had given the Okandas a virtual monopoly on river trade, and they were highly skilled at navigating the rapids. Brazzà noted that, unlike most of the other inland tribes, the Okandas had adopted many of the luxuries of the more sophisticated coastal peoples. Their woven garments were dyed in a variety of colors, and the Okandan women arranged their hair in elaborate styles that required several days to complete. Considering themselves by far the most attractive women in the region, the Okandan ladies used colored powders, lotions, and perfumes as the final touches in their beauty regimen.

While charmed and fascinated by some aspects of life in Africa, Brazzà was quite disheartened by others. As he wrote in a letter to his father, he was discouraged by the mediocre progress he had made in the area of freeing slaves. "I gave them freedom, but by now most of them have gone back to the very people who sold them to me. Out of thirteen slaves I bought, three had been sold into slavery by their fathers, three by their eldest brother, two by their younger brother and one by his uncle." Then again, given the antagonistic relations among many of the tribes, it is not entirely surprising that many former slaves eventually chose to return to their villages.

But Brazzà was heartened to learn that he was again financially solvent. In January 1877 his parents wired a credit of 4000 French francs to his suppliers in Libreville.

By March, Brazzà's strength had returned, and the weather was favorable. The annual February market in Lopé was over and many traders were leaving town to return to their villages and crops. Presenting the local chieftains with gifts in thanks for their months of hospitality, Brazzà had convinced them to let him gather the rest of his men and supplies and continue his explorations.

Before the departure of their honored guests, the chiefs performed a traditional ceremony to ensure the travelers the protection of the spirits. The head rower of each pirogue was given a small packet wrapped in leaves that contain seeds, animal claws, fur, and other items thought to possess magical powers. A handful of pebbles and earth was thrown into each boat. Brazzà completed the ceremony by setting off some of his remaining fireworks.

The Okandas seemed moved by his departure. "*Kenda na bouedi!*" or "Peace be with you!" the villagers cried, as

Brazzà and his fleet of 33 pirogues sailed off to begin their journey upriver.

Despite all the invocations to the spirits, during their passage through the rapids there were a few unfortunate incidents. At one point Brazzà's pirogue hit a rock and tipped over. No one was injured, but Brazzà saw his books, papers, maps, and navigational instruments tumble into the river. Hamon, the quartermaster, managed to salvage most of the items, which they let dry as best they could. A few days later, while the party slept on the bank, a sudden rise in the river level during the night sent two of their pirogues floating back downstream. The next morning some of the rowers, aided by local villagers, sailed back through the rapids, found the two boats intact, and brought them back to join the convoy.

They had nearly come to the end of the rapids when, seeing a whitish cloud of vapor hovering above the river ahead, the rowers stopped paddling and pointed at the cloud, crying "Booué! Booué!" Brazzà listened carefully and clearly heard the roar of the Booué Falls. It was one of the region's major cataracts, more than 150 feet wide and 20 feet high. Brazzà signaled the entire fleet to come to a halt at the riverbank. Everything would have to be unloaded and carried overland past the falls, including the enormous pirogues.

Fortunately the falls were near the village of one of the chiefs Brazzà had befriended earlier in the mission. Hearing of their plight, the chief had several hundred of his tribesmen help the French expedition transport everything to the calmer waters below the falls. It was a herculean task, expertly coordinated by Victor Hamon. To thank the tribesman Brazzà gave each of them a spoonful of salt, a rare and valuable commodity in the forest. Salt was so rare, in fact, that to preserve their food, many of the tribes used a substitute for salt derived from ashes.

Once past the rapids the expedition made better progress. Passing Zabouré's village, they stopped to greet him and to buy provisions. Finally, after weeks on the river under the blazing sun, Brazzà and his party were reunited with the rest of the mission in Doumé, where Ballay and Marche had established their new headquarters. It was the first day of April 1877. Brazzà had not seen Ballay and Marche for five months.

Brazzà and his men were now in the territory of the Adoumas. Despite their fearsome reputation among the neighboring tribes, the Adoumas welcomed the French expedition with open arms and gave them every consideration. After all, as long as the powerful white chief remained their guest, they had no fear of attacks from their hostile neighbors, and were able to trade for any goods they liked. Thus it was in their interest to have Brazzà stay with them as long as possible.

The young commander had in fact no other choice. All the Okandan rowers and freed slaves who had worked for him up until now had returned to their villages along the river. Even former slaves who knew that they would probably be re-sold into slavery were anxious to return home to show their families the trinkets they had acquired in other villages. None of them was at all interested in venturing into Adouma country.

The French mission was back to what it had been in Libreville: Brazzà, Ballay, Marche, Hamon, ten Senegalese marines, and four Gabonese interpreters. Denis, the most reliable and intelligent of the interpreters, also served as

Brazzà's cook, valet, and bodyguard. The large number of rowers they would need to proceed further up the Ogoway would have to be hired from among the Adoumas. As of now, all the Adouma villagers refused. To further discourage Brazzà's plans to leave Doumé, they regaled his Senegalese and Gabonese subordinates with frightening tales of what lay ahead. The Obambas and Oumbétés, they said, could disappear and reappear at will to trap and slaughter unsuspecting travelers. The Batekes did not speak, but sang like birds, and possessed magical knives that set fire to everything they touched. Hearing these stories, the marines and interpreters, already so far from home, began to feel worried and uncertain.

Brazzà considered these problems temporary. During his absence, Noël Ballay had gone on several reconnaissance trips in the region and assured him that the Ogoway was navigable at least up to the N'coni River. Brazzà decided that they would establish their next headquarters just past that point, near the Poubara Falls. Unfortunately a major calamity was brewing even as they made these plans. The Okandan rowers had apparently become infected with smallpox, and the disease was spreading through all the villages to which they had returned. Although Brazzà and his men showed no sign of smallpox, they were blamed for its arrival. Tales spread that Brazzà was an evil wizard, and that in a fit of anger he had released the illness with the fireworks he had set off in Lopé. Some said that the white man carried many diseases in those large crates of his, and that all he had to do was to open them up to infect a village with the plague of his choice.

Brazzà realized that all he could do was wait until the epidemic had run its course. Meanwhile the tribesmen reasoned that if the white men brought the disease, then they must have the means to cure it. They soon came to Doumé to ask the explorers for a remedy, and Ballay conscientiously visited every patient he could. The young doctor found that most cases responded readily to treatment, but the problem was to get the villagers to follow the proper procedures. As he noted later in an article published in the Paris Geographical Society's bulletin, the traditional native remedy for such a disease was to have the patient bathe in the cold water of the river, and to apply ointments to the skin eruptions. In some cases, very ill patients were ostracized and left to die in the forest. Ballay's challenge was to convince the villagers that the patient needed to be kept in a closed hut, where a small fire kept the air at a constant warm temperature. When the villagers followed these and a few other simple procedures, they soon saw their patients recovering. By June 15th, the epidemic was largely over.

Brazzà spent his long stay in Doumé observing life in the village, as was his usual custom, and writing detailed descriptions of everything he saw. He noted that the Adoumas were excellent weavers. Their cloth made from raffia fiber was highly prized, as was their mosquito netting. They also produced fine baskets, straw mats, hunting nets from vine fiber, and fishing nets from pineapple fiber. They worked metal to produce axes, knives, and various tools. Although they were less talented than their neighbors at maneuvering boats, they built some of the best pirogues Brazzà had ever seen. Carved out of huge tree trunks, Adouma pirogues were as large as four feet wide and sixty feet long, and could carry up to 3000 pounds of merchandise.

By the end of June, Brazzà had convinced the Adouma chiefs to permit him to hire several hundred rowers in exchange for a varied list of items. Each rower would receive fabric, salt, gunpowder, a knife, a mirror, a handkerchief, a bowl, some glass beads, etc.; each chief would receive a rifle, a copper basin, some clothing, jewelry, etc. The merchandise was made ready, but as usual, the Adoumas kept finding pretexts to prevent Brazzà's departure. The young ensign realized that a ruse would be necessary if he were ever to leave Doumé.

Brazzà and his men repacked their supplies into smaller containers, leaving a number of empty crates "in storage" in the Adouma camp. On July 1st, Ballay and Hamon began heading upstream with most of the staff and, unbeknownst to the Adoumas, all of the remaining supplies. Brazzà followed them on July 22nd with his last few men, just as the Adoumas were discovering that the crates he had "stored" with them were empty.

The following month on the Ogoway was an alternation of peaceful days on the river's wide expanses, watching the changing landscape while the rowers chanted and sang their tribal songs, and exhausting days of maneuvering through the rapids, punctuated by the usual accidents and incidents. Along their route, the expedition received a cordial welcome from the Obamba chieftain Libossi and from many other chiefs. On August 6, 1877 the mission reached the confluence of the M'passa River, and that evening they arrived at Machongo, nearly six hundred miles from the Gabonese coast. Beyond this point, the Ogoway narrowed into a series of waterfalls and rapids, and was no longer navigable.

Brazzà and his men set up their camp on a hill where they had a wide view of the surrounding countryside. Brazzà realized that he had been wrong about the Ogoway. It was neither the great river that flowed to the lakes of East Africa, nor a direct route to the center of the continent. He shared his thoughts with Noël Ballay, who asked him if their mission was now over.

"Not at all," responded Brazzà. Although the Ogoway had not fulfilled their expectations, it was not their only objective. They had come to Africa to try to solve the mystery of what lay between the Gabonese coast and the rivers and lakes of the east, and Brazzà was still ready and willing to do so. These first two years of exploration had taught them much, and had given them the skills they would need to advance further. Brazzà and his men had come to know the Africans and their ways, and they had learned to survive under the most challenging of conditions. More exciting discoveries could lie ahead of them.

But did his companions feel the same way? Would they continue to follow him? Ballay and Hamon agreed without hesitation. Alfred Marche, however, decided to turn back. He had ample reasons to do so: two years of privations, illness, malnutrition, and exhausting marches. Furthermore, he was neither an explorer nor a diplomat; he was a naturalist.

But the real motivation for his departure may have originated in his disposition and his relationship with Brazzà. Despite his considerable skills, knowledge, and endurance, Marche had often shown his temper during this mission. He did not have the friendly, easy rapport with the tribesmen that had been such an asset to Brazzà, Ballay, and Hamon. There was also the fact that Marche was eight years older than Brazzà, his commander, and Marche could very possibly have harbored feelings of envy toward the young ensign. Soon after Marche's return to France, he published an article in the popular magazine *Le Tour du Monde* detailing his experiences along the Ogoway, but giving Brazzà only one cursory mention, as if the leader had played only a minor role in the expedition.

As for the Senegalese marines and the interpreters, they were hesitant to leave the relative safety of the river for totally unknown, and possibly uninhabited, territory, but Brazzà managed to convince them to stay with the mission. Meanwhile the rainy season was beginning, making any new expedition theoretically impossible. A few days later, quartermaster Hamon was checking through the inventory when he made an unpleasant discovery. The supposedly watertight crate that held their entire supply of shoes had in fact been taking on water ever since the first few shipwrecks on the Ogoway. All the shoes were rotted through!

How long would they have to go barefoot? Weeks, maybe months? "The barefoot conquerors!" thought Brazzà sardonically. Then he remembered that years earlier in Senegal, the marines had quoted an African proverb warning that people who wore shoes could not be trusted. Well, perhaps this piece of bad luck would help endear them to the next few tribes they met!

The following week, despite the wind and rainstorms and the stifling heat, Brazzà set off to reconnoiter the M'passa with a staff limited to Denis and a few rowers. Beyond the Ogoway, however, the dialects changed completely and Denis could no longer serve as an interpreter, so Brazzà hired another. Traveling up the M'passa they were welcomed in several villages. Brazzà was quite impressed to see a magnificent suspension bridge made of braided vines with wooden supports. Where had the extremely isolated Ondoumbo tribe learned this great engineering skill, he wondered.

For their part, the Ondoumbos seemed amazed that Brazzà wished to go past their territory into Bateke country. The Batekes were a strange people who spoke a bizarre, incomprehensible language, said the Ondoumbos. Their land was barren, baked by the sun during the day, and freezing by night. But after a few days of bargaining, Brazzà managed to hire two Ondoumbo guides to escort him to the land of the Batekes.

In late March they arrived in Bateke territory, and Brazzà noted a distinct change in the landscape. The lush vegetation of the equatorial forest was gone. Here the soil was sandy and dry, in some places giving way to grassy savannahs. The small expedition traveled much more quickly than they had in the forest, but suffered acutely from the lack of water. Here the rivers were few and far between. The men had to take shelter from the burning sun during the day, but as the Ondoumbos had told Brazzà, the temperature dropped dramatically at night. The cool, almost wintry early morning air invigorated the travelers. They made good progress, despite the fact that they were not only barefoot but clothed in tatters, after weeks of hiking through the thorny underbrush.

In this flat, open country, they could see trees and villages a long way off. The Batekes also had ample warning of their arrival, and prepared a ceremonial welcome for the unusual visitor and his party. Although the Batekes occasionally sent their merchants to trade for European manufactured goods, which were well known to them and highly prized, it was virtually unheard of for a white traveler simply to show up at their village.

Brazzà's arrival provoked quite a stir. Children hid behind their mothers, and even the men, armed with long traditional knives and poisoned darts, stood at a respectful distance. Brazzà was fascinated by the Batekes' clothing, ornaments, and weapons, but he took care to observe discreetly. A sudden glance or abrupt movement on his part would have frightened everyone.

N'jayolé, the chief, had donned his ceremonial attire, which included a large, woven headdress that looked like a horned helmet. He laid gifts of salt, beads, and fabric before Brazzà. After a pause he announced to the white chief in a very proud tone, "The lands that you have just left are poor lands. They have nothing. Their gifts are manioc, bananas, corn, chickens, sheep, and slaves. We Batekes, superior to these savages, are happy to offer you the things that come from your country."

Tired and hungry, Brazzà would gladly have accepted the chicken and the manioc, but he understood that the Batekes' primary concern was to make a good impression. He presented N'jayolé and his fellow chiefs with gifts. They seemed satisfied, but according to Bateke tradition, the guests were not offered food until nightfall.

During the next few days Brazzà saw fields of manioc, sugar cane, tobacco, and other crops, evidence of the intensive agriculture of this sandy, seemingly infertile land. Although the Batekes raised enough food for their needs, their land did not produce the abundant harvests of the forest tribes. For this reason the Batekes did not stay primarily within their own territory, as did the Ondoumbos, but traveled throughout the surrounding countryside and knew it well. Unlike the tribes Brazzà had visited previously, however, the Batekes were very cautious and generally unwilling to give information.

Brazzà returned to Machongo in September where he rejoined Ballay and Hamon and told them of his plan to move their headquarters to Bateke country. Engaging porters wherever they could, they settled in an uninhabited region in the midst of the eastern tribes, creating a neutral area where they could have contact with everyone. Over the course of the winter they noticed that various tribes took advantage of the neutral French camp to trade with normally hostile neighbors.

Brazzà and his men waited out the rainy season, concentrating on maintaining their health and stocking up on food supplies. The beginning of 1878 saw them moving eastward on foot. When they reached the Alima River, about 160 miles from Machongo, Brazzà was struck by the transparency of its water, which contrasted sharply with its marshy riverbanks. He could see all the way to the bottom of this river, which was nearly 20 feet deep. What was the source of this fresh, clear water?

The aged chief of a neighboring village gave them the answer. He said that not far off flowed a much larger river, whose course went north, then east. "Many pirogues sail on it," said the old chief. "People from far regions come to trade with the tribes along its banks." He described a great expanse of water, and Brazzà wondered if this larger river communicated with the vast interior lake that most European geographers assumed lay at the center of the African continent.

Then the old chief showed them a kind of black salt that resembled samples that explorers of east Africa had brought back to Europe. To Brazzà this proved that there was a water route of some kind that crossed central Africa, linking the Alima to the east coast. But he did not suspect that he was only about 100 miles from the heart of this route, the river Congo.

Brazzà and his companions were anxious to explore the Alima River, but for the first time on this mission, they had doubts about their safety along the way. The Batekes cautioned them about the fearsome Apfourou tribe who controlled the Alima, and this time Brazzà sensed that the warning was more than just rhetoric motivated by intertribal bickering. The Apfourous had an aggressive and warlike reputation, and they had beaten every tribe that had come into contact with them. Could Brazzà possibly win their friendship?

It was now June 1878. Brazzà and his men began their trip down the Alima, proceeding slowly and watching for signs of life along the banks. When they came to the first village, Brazzà stepped ashore and looked around. The settlement was deserted, and looked as if the villagers had just dropped everything and fled. Brazzà took a little food, and left a generous pile of merchandise in exchange, as a sign of his goodwill.

The next village the mission passed was not only inhabited, but welcoming. Brazzà met with the Apfourou chieftains. They seemed receptive, and even agreed to sell him another pirogue. Encouraged by their friendliness, Brazzà and his men sailed further down the river.

But there had been a serious misunderstanding. The Apfourous had agreed to the French explorer's traveling on "their" river, but not to his transporting merchandise. That privilege was reserved for them. After passing a few more villages, Brazzà and his men were surprised to hear war cries upstream, then downstream. Pirogues full of Apfourou warriors were coming towards them from both sides.

Caught in an ambush, the explorers had no choice but to defend themselves with their rifles. When the skirmish was over and the Apfourous had retreated, the French expedition, shaken but unhurt, took refuge along the bank. At nightfall, they saw fires being lit up and down the river. Apparently the entire Apfourou tribe was gathering for a massacre!

"We could hear our enemies chanting that we were the meat for their victory banquet," wrote Brazzà. He instructed his men to dig in as best they could. They barely had enough weapons and ammunition to defend themselves from a major siege, and certainly not enough to attack or to make further progress down the river. Brazzà's mission of exploration was over; that was clear. But for now, all he and his men could do was to try to hold off the attack.

The Apfourou assault began at dawn. Thanks to their superior weapons and sharpshooters, the French camp managed to repel the Apfourous a second time. For the moment Brazzà and his men were safe, but they were profoundly demoralized.

"I'll never forget that warrior in the front of his pirogue," said Brazzà.

Hamon shook his head. "Neither will I. He came right into our fire and kept standing the whole time."

"He waved a talisman above his head, and that seemed to protect him from the bullets that were raining all around him," continued Brazzà.

They realized that the Apfourous would be back, and that this temporary respite was their best chance to escape. Brazzà and his men abandoned all but the most essential items, even if it meant leaving some of the scientific equipment. At nightfall, most of the expedition headed out on foot, protected by a rear guard who followed later. By the smoky light of bamboo torches, they spent the next three hours fleeing barefoot through a *poto-poto*, or swamp, and then over the hills. By the next evening, they had made it safely back to Bateke territory.

It was now July 1878, nearly three years since they had left France for a mission that had been allotted six months! Brazzà saw that his expedition could go no further. His men were exhausted and many were ill. And yet, there was one month left in the dry season, and the indefatigable Brazzà was determined to do a little bit more exploring. He decided to send Hamon back to the coast with the sick, while Ballay and the others waited for him at Machongo. Brazzà himself would go on one last foray with six marines and ten porters.

Exhausted, in poor health, barefoot, and in rags, Brazzà was still fascinated by everything he saw. He visited more villages, heard more dialects, saw more new and interesting plants and foodstuffs. But a week or so into August 1878, he and his companions heard the birdsong that signaled the beginning of the rainy season, and this time even Brazzà realized it was time to turn back. Soon wind and rain would make a return trip impossible. Looking at himself, he saw that his legs were covered with sores. Looking at his followers, he saw that he had driven them to the point where they could barely walk. On August 11th, they began their long trek back to the coast.

Near Machongo, they met up with Ballay and his men. The porters were returning to their villages, and Brazzà, Ballay, and the remaining marines and interpreters boarded pirogues and began their last descent of the Ogoway rapids. At least this time they were headed downstream, making the ordeal a little easier. As the Frenchmen passed familiar villages, they were greeted by friends who offered them food and wished them well. Brazzà made gifts of the last of the merchandise.

The journey seemed successful until they were near the end of the rapids, when a hippo struck Ballay's pirogue, sending it whirling into the rushing river. The ensign came to his doctor's aid and they managed to right the small craft, though Brazzà lost his watch and his compass in the process.

Their arrival in Libreville was a time not of joy, but of mourning. Denis Dolimnie, Brazzà's faithful interpreter, had died of exhaustion. The explorer had known him for six years; they had met at the time of Brazzà's naval duty as a midshipman off the Gabon coast. Now, at the age of 25, a year younger than Brazzà himself, Denis was gone. Along with all the other indelible experiences of the mission, this loss would be a powerful reminder of the consequences of the young commander's decisions.

In November 1878, exactly three years after their arrival in Libreville, Brazzà and his companions boarded the *Pioneer*, the naval transport that would take them back to France. The two-month voyage gave Brazzà ample time to look back on his recent experiences, and to make his way through the sack of mail he had received at the French naval station in Libreville.

In among the letters were reports of the most recent European explorations of Africa, including Stanley's *Through the Dark Continent*. Brazzà immediately plunged into this riveting account of Stanley's journey from the Indian Ocean to the Atlantic, and he soon realized that the Anglo-American explorer had given him the one piece of information he needed to crack the mystery of the central African river system. Stanley had followed the course of a huge waterway that he had named "the Livingstone" and that the various African tribes called the Lualaba, the Nzere, or the Congo. This was the "great water" of which the old African chief had spoken! Here was the source of the Alima's clear water, and of the black sand from East Africa! The Alima was obviously a tributary of the Congo.

Now it all seemed simple. The Congo, despite its importance to the inland tribes, was impractical as a trade route to the Atlantic because of the massive series of rapids over its last 200 miles. Combining Stanley's description of the Congo with Brazzà's own knowledge of the Ogoway, the Alima, and the overland crossings between them, the French explorer realized that a navigable route across Africa did exist.

And right now he, Brazzà, was the only one who knew it.

CHAPTER SIX -- THE EXPLORER

On January 6, 1879, the *Pioneer* dropped anchor at Bordeaux. As Brazzà boarded the train to Paris, the sight of French travelers dressed warmly for the bracing winter weather enhanced the contrast between France and the equatorial African bush, where he had spent the past three eventful years. France was industrializing rapidly, and after the slow pace of life in the tropics, everyone Brazzà saw seemed to be in a hurry.

In Paris, a grandiose new City Hall was being built to replace the one that had been incinerated during the civil strife of the Commune in 1871. Charles Garnier's magnificent opera house, now the centerpiece of the capital's grand boulevards, was entertaining the cream of Parisian society. The city had recently hosted a successful World's Fair at the newly-built Trocadero Palace, which architect Eugène Viollet-Le-Duc was now transforming into a museum of monumental architecture.

Paris was expanding in every direction. Churches, hospitals, schools, and entire neighborhoods were being planned and built. There were several new bridges spanning the Seine. The new Grenelle Bridge would later be graced with a scale model of the monumental statue "Liberty

Lighting the World" that France presented to the United States in honor of the young nation's centennial in 1876.

Twenty-seven-year-old Brazzà, emaciated but still tall, dark, and handsome, was warmly welcomed by his friends at the *Petite Vache*, where he now took his place as one of the experienced explorers. Besides all the excitement and adventure it had brought him, his expedition had accomplished much. His careful notes and hand-drawn plans were filling in the "blank spaces" on European maps of equatorial Africa with previously unknown rivers, mountains, and other natural features. Many new species of animals and plants had been discovered. Noël Ballay had done important research on tropical diseases and possible methods of prevention. In years to come, Brazzà's descriptions of African tribes and their customs would help stimulate the development of the new discipline of anthropology.

In recognition of his contributions to science and geography, Brazzà was to receive several prestigious awards, including the French Republic's Legion of Honor, the Sorbonne's Academic Palms, and the Paris Geographical Society's Gold Medal. He was invited to give speeches not only in France, but also in Italy and Great Britain. The young ensign felt extremely honored, but one ardent desire still glowed in his heart: to be entrusted with a second mission to Africa.

If Brazzà was to make a good impression at all these events, his most pressing need at the moment was proper attire. Admiral de Montaignac insisted that he meet Aristide Boucicaut, owner of the Left Bank's fashionable new department store, *Le Bon Marché*. Brazzà was welcomed to the emporium in style, and he selected all the clothing an elegant Parisian gentleman might require. Boucicaut would not hear of Brazzà's paying the bill. *Le Bon Marché* was proud to present the purchases as a gift to France's distinguished young explorer.

But not everyone in Paris was so impressed. Montaignac no longer presided over the Ministry of the Navy, where Brazzà now learned he had more than his share of detractors. The charismatic, foreign-born Count of Brazzà was the center of much publicity and attention, and at 27 he was already receiving coveted honors that had eluded French naval officers twice his age.

Brazzà was aware of the envy engendered by his success, and he could not ignore it. The second mission to Africa that he so keenly desired would have to be approved by many of his superior officers. Brazzà, now promoted to lieutenant junior grade, would have to try to maintain good relationships with as many people as he could.

As he had done to gain support for his first mission, Brazzà thought carefully about whom he could interest in his latest project, and how he should appeal to them. Once again he attended Parisian parties and receptions, many of which were now given in his honor. He captivated the scientific community with the wealth of natural discoveries that awaited European explorers in Africa. When speaking to wealthy businessmen, he stressed the value of African natural resources like ivory and rubber, and the potential of new markets eager to trade for European products. Little did he suspect that only a decade later, the European stampede for rubber would degenerate into a massacre.

Brazzà diligently visited powerful political contacts like Léon Gambetta, Jules Ferry, and Ferdinand de Lesseps to discuss the importance of France's presence in Africa. Above all, he revealed to certain strategically selected naval officers and statesmen that he had discovered the only navigable river route into central Africa, and that this precious itinerary could be under the sole control of the French, if Brazzà was sent back to Africa in time. He had established good relations with the tribes in the region, and had given them a favorable impression of the French. Now Brazzà was ready to solidify his country's gains by signing treaties with the tribal rulers and setting up French settlements along the desired route.

Exotic, remote, and inaccessible as it seemed, Africa was soon to become Europe's favorite chessboard. Bitter rivalries and unresolved disputes that had simmered for centuries between Britain and France, France and Prussia, Belgium and its larger, more powerful neighbors, in short between nearly every pair of neighboring countries and one-time enemies in Europe, would now be reignited on African soil, at the expense of a population who knew little and cared less about these distant northern lands. In the decades to follow, the Europeans' mad rush for African colonies would be known by the undignified and entirely accurate name of "the Scramble for Africa."

Motives behind the Scramble were many and varied: the need for military bases and support stations, the economic advantages of new raw materials and markets, the prestige of flying one's flag over a faraway nation and imposing one's language and customs on its people, and, of course, missionary zeal to propagate the Christian faith. A large number of Europeans were convinced that they were performing a valuable service to "primitive" peoples by endowing them not only with what they considered the one true religion, but also with a highly-developed culture.

The French, for example, considered their language, literature, cuisine, and technology the finest in the world, and therefore precious gifts for any nation. Many present-day Americans learning about life in developing countries would feel exactly the same way about spreading the culture, educational methods, and scientific advances of the United States.

What motivated Pierre Savorgnan de Brazzà as he became a more and more important player in Europe's great colonial enterprise? His personal drive had not changed since childhood: he was drawn to adventure and the unknown. In a way, his career in the French Navy could have seemed merely a convenient way to satisfy this longing for adventure, since he spent relatively little time serving in traditional naval assignments.

At the same time, Brazzà was patriotic, and from the day he was granted French nationality to the day he died, his fidelity to his adopted country never wavered. Every discovery he made was for the greater glory of France, and for no other nation or entity.

Lastly, Brazzà's interest in Africa and its people grew stronger with every mission, despite all the hardships and illnesses he endured during his travels there. He sincerely believed that a colonial "partnership," as he saw it, and the greatly increased trade it would bring, could be a source of revenue, prosperity, and development for Africa. His method of patient diplomacy and cooperation with the African tribes, combined with his respect for their traditions and customs, seemed to be working, and he was convinced that he could establish not only a colony but an entire colonial system along those lines. In reality, his efforts would only help provoke one of modern history's major catastrophes.

Of course, Brazzà was far from being the only famous traveler of the day. Ever since Henry Morton Stanley had located the ailing missionary Dr. Livingstone by the shores of Lake Tanganyika in 1871, the Anglo-American explorer had become an international star. The Paris Geographical Society, who would present their 1879 Gold Medal for distinguished exploration to Brazzà, had bestowed the previous year's honor on Stanley. There was even a Stanley Club in Paris for his many French supporters.

What impressed Europeans most about the Welsh-born journalist-turned-adventurer was the amazing amount of territory he covered. Between 1874 and 1877, Stanley and his armed force of 350 people crossed the entire African continent from east to west, tracing the course of the Congo River over a distance of 1500 miles. Not inclined to waste his time in diplomatic discussions, Stanley simply shot anyone who got in his way. Unlike Brazzà, who considered himself not a conqueror but a guest in foreign territory, Stanley viewed Africa as uninhabited, as a vast vacant lot ready to be claimed by white entrepreneurs. While the French officer's journals and letters were full of descriptions of tribal rites and customs, Stanley's papers contained endless lists of topographical measurements and statistics, by which he intended to prove the immense potential of his conquest.

Although their methods and motivations were diametrically opposed, Brazzà professed great admiration for Stanley. As did all Europeans, the Frenchman owed much of his knowledge of central African geography to his Anglo-American colleague's relentless marches. In his 1887 book *Conférences et lettres*, Brazzà refers to Stanley as "Africa's most intrepid explorer."

Apart from Africa itself, the only place where Stanley was unpopular was precisely where he longed to be accepted: in Britain. In his land of origin, Stanley still bore the stigma of the words written on his birth certificate, "John Rowlands, bastard." Although he had changed his name, traveled the world, and become a famed newspaper correspondent, Stanley remained in the British view little more than a profiteer and a pirate. The British government's lack of interest in his discoveries and its refusal to sponsor his next expedition deepened the wounds that had festered in him since childhood.

In the late 1870s, Britain was in no great need of new colonies, as she was already the acknowledged leader in Europe's colonial sweepstakes. Her possessions extended from Canada through the Middle East, to India, Malaysia, and Australia. The other European powers were, of course, anxious to keep up with Britain, and no ruler felt this need more acutely than Leopold II, King of the Belgians.

Disdainful of his own small nation, and resentful of Europeans' growing demands for democratic governments at the expense of monarchies like his own, Leopold sought a colony that he could rule and exploit as despotically as he chose. After trying to purchase colonies in Asia and South America, Leopold began following Stanley's progress in Africa. He realized with delight that most of this vast continent was still unknown to, and unclaimed by, Europeans. The more he heard about Stanley's forced marches and brutal methods, the more interested the King became. As surely as Stanley had found Livingstone, Leopold had found his man.

Humanitarian and anti-slavery organizations had considerable public support in Europe throughout the 19th century, and the Belgian monarch was well aware that if he was to gain the kind of immense profits he desired, he would need to cover his tracks. In 1876 he gathered a prestigious group of noted missionaries and explorers to a well-publicized Geographical Conference in Brussels, where he established a nominally philanthropic organization, the International African Association. The Association was composed of an international committee in Brussels, and national committees in all the major European countries. Together, proposed Leopold, these committees would collect and disburse funds to build roads and establish clinics and laboratories in the little-known territories of central Africa. The Association seemed entirely respectable and even had its own flag, adorned with a gold star on a blue background. Leopold received great praise for his ambitious altruistic endeavor.

When Stanley returned to Europe in late 1877 after making his way across Africa, the Belgian monarch was determined to hire him. Here was the explorer who could bring Leopold's long-held dream of a vast colony to fruition. In the summer and autumn of 1878, Stanley accepted the King's invitations to his royal palaces in Brussels and Laeken. Dazzled by the regal receptions he received, particularly after his rejection by the British Crown, Stanley agreed to return to the Congo to establish bases for the International African Association, and to build a road through the Crystal Mountains to the point above the rapids where the Congo River became navigable. The road and river passages would allow Leopold to transport ivory and other valuable natural resources to the coast, where they could enter European commerce.

In this huge undertaking, Leopold would provide Stanley with a generous salary, and with all the men and equipment he required. Above all, the political and economic aims of the mission were to be kept secret, and Stanley would leave Europe under the name of Mr. Henri. A five-year contract was signed by both parties, and by February 1879, Stanley was on his way back to Africa

Hearing of Brazzà's return to Paris after a three-year exploration of the mysterious Ogoway region, Leopold considered hiring the Frenchman as well. Young explorers always needed money, and the monarch assumed that he could easily persuade Brazzà to transfer his allegiance from the French Navy to the International African Association.

In July of 1879, Brazzà was in the fashionable French spa town of Vichy, recovering from bronchitis and a liver problem. When he received an invitation to visit the King of the Belgians to receive the honorific "Leopold Medal," the young explorer assumed it was another courtesy visit.

In August, arriving at the royal residence of Laeken on the outskirts of Brussels, Brazzà was received warmly by the King. After the medal had been presented, Leopold came quickly to the real point of the visit, and invited Brazzà to lead a mission for the Association.

Surprised, Brazzà responded, "Sire, I am a French officer. If your majesty desires my services, he will have to make a request to my country's government."

Leopold impatiently dismissed his answer. "We could do great things together! I'll make a fortune out of the Congo."

Respectful but grave, Brazzà repeated that he was a French naval officer. Unused to opposition of any kind, the Belgian King began to lose his temper. With a disparaging glance at the lieutenant's dress uniform, he scoffed, "Do you really mean that you are going to let those little stripes of yours stand in the way of the brilliant career I can offer you?"

Brazzà remained silent. Raised as an Italian nobleman in a Roman palazzo, he was not subject to Stanley's vulnerabilities and desperate need for royal recognition. He would behave courteously to the Belgian King and accept his hospitality for another few days, but he would not be manipulated. Whether the young lieutenant realized it or not, he had just made a rich, powerful enemy for life.

Before leaving Belgium, Brazzà learned from a foreign diplomat that the International African Association was in no way the philanthropic organization it professed to be. It was simply a screen for Leopold's greedy plan for a highly profitable central African colony. In fact, the Association was already moribund, and was giving way to two more questionable entities backed by Leopold, the Committee for Studies of the Upper Congo, and the International Association of the Congo. Behind all these names lurked the rapacious ambition of the Belgian King, who had just sent Stanley back to Africa to build roads and establish bases for the eventual exploitation of the equatorial forest.

With the revelation of these evil schemes dominating his thoughts, Brazzà returned to Paris. He knew that if allowed to proceed unopposed, Stanley would claim the entire Congo basin for the Belgian monarch, who respected no law. But under the flag of France, a republic with a tradition of human rights, the tribes of Gabon and Congo would have a chance at decency and prosperity.

By now, the autumn of 1879, Stanley had already arrived at the Congo Estuary, but Brazzà knew that dynamiting his way through the mountains to build a road around the lower Congo rapids would take Stanley at least a year. That would allow Brazzà time to pursue his proposed route from the French stations on the Gabonese coast down the Ogoway to the Alima, and along the Alima to the great River Congo. There Brazzà could plant the French flag and safeguard the territory west of the river for France.

More motivated than ever, the 27-year-old lieutenant continued his appeals to politicians, to the business community, and to the French public to entrust him with another mission to equatorial Africa. To increase his chances for approval, he requested only a minimum of funds.

In November, his proposal for a second mission was approved. He was granted 100,000 francs, a far cry from the millions that backed Stanley. King Leopold, who refused to give up on Brazzà, had the French Committee of his International African Association credit the mission with another 50,000 francs, theoretically to select locations for two scientific and medical stations. This amount would serve, Leopold hoped, to remind Brazzà of the limitless budget that still awaited him if he ever lost patience with the French navy.

The financial backing was also a way to insure that Leopold would continue to hear news of Brazzà. Since the contribution was from a "humanitarian" association, Brazzà could not refuse it without creating a scandal that would embarrass everyone involved, including himself. Besides, he needed the money. As always, the explorer's parents wired a generous financial contribution from Rome.

Accompanied by Joseph Michaud, one of the French navy's mechanical engineers, Brazzà embarked at Liverpool on December 27, 1879. Although he was not traveling under a false name as had Stanley, Brazzà too was on a secret mission: to reach central Africa's greatest river before his rival.

CHAPTER SEVEN ~ THE CHALLENGER

Brazzà's first mission to Africa had been a loosely-defined expedition into the *terra incognita* around the Ogoway River. In some ways it had been a journey of self-discovery, motivated entirely by Brazzà's own curiosity, fed by his enthusiasm, and brought to its completion by his charismatic leadership style. Three years in the African bush had taught him much about the land and its people. He hoped to use that knowledge as he began his second mission, one with much more precise goals.

Ostensibly, Brazzà was returning to equatorial Africa to do some further topographical research for the French government and to choose the sites for two proposed hospitals, one along the Ogoway, and another along the Congo. If he didn't manage to reach the Congo River before Stanley had claimed both banks for the Belgian king, the second mission would be limited to those tasks.

Brazzà's goals would be different, however, if he was the first to arrive at Malebo Pool, the vast, tranquil expanse where the Congo gathered its waters before plunging into the long series of rapids that flowed into the Atlantic. By the shores of the basin that the intrepid Anglo-American had recently named "Stanley Pool" after himself, the young lieutenant hoped to plant the French flag on the right bank of the great river, and establish his country's claim with a treaty of friendship signed in due form by the local ruler. Unlike his rival, Brazzà had neither the means nor the desire to force his way through Gabon and Congo at gunpoint.

In January 1880, Brazzà arrived in Senegal, where he engaged ten marines and a corporal to command them. The corporal was a Senegalese of Moorish-Berber origin named Malamine Kemara, and he would become one of Brazzà's most loyal and essential subordinates. During the passage south from Senegal to Gabon, Brazzà had an opportunity to get to know Malamine, who was a responsible and intelligent leader. Respected by his men, the corporal was fluent in French and several African languages and dialects, and was a crack rifle shot and an expert hunter. He would later be known among the tribesmen by the nickname *Mayele*, meaning "clever" or "cunning."

Brazzà's principal staff for the second expedition was now in place. Besides Malamine and the ten marines, he would be assisted by the French naval engineers Michaud and Noguez. Ballay, who had now completed his medical degree, would join them later with a shipment of several dismantled steamboats to be re-assembled on site.

Libreville was festive at Brazzà's return. Tom-toms conveyed news of his arrival from village to village, and he was greeted with music and feasting. A few of the slaves he had freed in the course of his first mission had settled in Libreville and were now proficient enough in French to serve as his interpreters. Brazzà was also able to rehire many of his former porters. He remembered that one of the major problems during his first mission had been the constant need to change rowers, since many tribesmen had refused to go beyond the territory ruled by their own chief. As a result it had taken Brazzà two years to reach the Upper Ogoway! This time, he hired only rowers who agreed to take him all the way to his destination.

Since time was of the essence, Brazzà and his men were traveling relatively lightly. He had already established friendly relations with many tribal chiefs, and would not need to spend months enjoying their hospitality and exchanging as many gifts as he had before. In Libreville Brazzà purchased the necessary pirogues and some additional local food supplies, and on March 8, 1880, his mission began its journey up the Ogoway. In only three months, they passed Lambarene, Lopé, and the Booué and Doumé Falls, and in June they arrived at the confluence of the Ogoway and Mpassa Rivers.

This strategic point at the meeting of two waterways was a good place for the first French scientific and medical station. The local Bateke tribe was in favor of the idea, since they viewed the Europeans' presence as a safeguard against aggressive acts from their troublesome neighbors. Recent intertribal conflicts had become so violent that the chief had ordered the construction of a new village at a safer distance from the neighboring tribe. Considering the presence of the white men as a guarantee of peace, however, the chief decided that his people would remain in their current settlement at Nghimi. He agreed to sell the recently-begun new village of a few huts and fields to the French explorers for their station.

As Brazzà prepared to found his first French settlement in Africa, he gave some thought to an appropriate name. He remembered how significant the name of Libreville, "city of the free," had always been to him. In French, a freed slave was referred to as an *affranchi*, or a "freedman." This place would be called Francheville, or "city of the freed."

On June 13, 1880, the local chiefs were invited to witness the founding of the new settlement. The French flag was raised with a salute of ten musket volleys. Calling his men to attention, Brazzà proclaimed, "In the name of France, here I plant our flag. *Vive la France, vive la république!* May God protect Francheville, the first French station founded in west central Africa."

Brazzà was proud, happy, and full of good intentions. In an ironic development that was not without its portents, however, Francheville soon became known as Franceville, or "city of the French." It was under that name that, in decades to come, the growing town would witness the increasingly somber events of its history.

Assuming that by June, Dr. Ballay had probably arrived at Libreville with the steamboats, Brazzà sent Michaud at the head of a fleet of pirogues back to the coast to bring Ballay and the equipment up the Ogoway. Leaving Noguez in charge of the new settlement, Brazzà set off with Malamine and Ossiah, their interpreter, along with five marines and a dozen porters. The small party headed southeast, in search of the great river. Brazzà knew that at some point he would eventually run into the Apfourous, the tribe of fierce warriors that had brought his first expedition to such an abrupt end, but, fixing his mind on his successful relations with all the other tribes, he remained confident that he could somehow manage to become friends with them as well.

Traveling on foot over the sandy, treeless inland plateau, they were received as guests by friendly tribes. An Aboma chieftain spoke to Brazzà about the great river, which he called the Olumo, and about King Makoko, a powerful ruler to whom most tribes in the region owed allegiance. Brazzà determined that the nearby Lefini River in Aboma territory was another tributary of the Congo. The explorers set about building a raft to take them down the Lefini to the all-important Congo.

No sooner had they started down the Lefini when they saw a pirogue approaching. In it was a chief, wearing the distinctive metal collar of Makoko's vassals. He brought Brazzà a message, and addressed the young lieutenant with respect. "For a long time Makoko has known of the great white chief of the Ogoway. He knows that his fearsome rifles have never been used to attack, and that peace and abundance accompany his steps. He has sent me to bring you his word of peace, and to guide you as his friend."

Brazzà was more than pleased at these welcome words, but he remained cautious. Through his interpreter Ossiah, he requested that on their way to see King Makoko, the envoy show him "the great water," or the River Congo. It was agreed, and the French party's raft began following their host's pirogue down the Lefini.

At a village called Ngampo, they went ashore and the envoy led them overland through a dry, uninhabited savannah. After two days' difficult march under the blazing sun, during which the guide seemed to lose his way several times, Brazzà could not help but suspect foul play. Was this a trap? He had Ossiah inform the envoy that his patience was wearing thin, and that if this was an ambush or trick, it would have serious consequences. But Makoko's vassal assured the French lieutenant that he would soon see "the great water."

Late the same night, after another long march, Brazzà and his men suddenly saw the silvery glimmer of a large expanse of water. Under the glowing moon, the Congo was as wide as a sea, and its calm waters flowed majestically towards the shadowy mountains in the distance. The quiet beauty of the memorable scene inspired what Brazzà would later call "a religious silence." His heart beat fast as he realized that the destiny of his mission would be decided here.

After calculating their precise location with the aid of stars and sextant, Brazzà and his men camped for the night. The next morning, they set off with their guide toward Makoko's royal village at a place called Mbé. Just beyond Mbé was the territory of Makoko's allies, the fierce Apfourou.

To facilitate his expedition's future progress, and to make an even more favorable impression on Makoko, Brazzà thought it best to resolve any problems with his redoubtable former enemies as soon as possible. In any case, the Apfourous controlled all trade in ivory and other merchandise on the upper Congo between the Alima and the Pool, and if the French were to establish a presence along the great river, they would need the Apfourous' support and cooperation.

The chief who had been guiding the party agreed to serve as an intermediary. During the two-day hike to Mbé, Brazzà discussed his diplomatic strategy with the chief and with Ossiah, who besides his familiarity with all the dialects of the Ogoway and lower Congo, possessed an invaluable knowledge of tribal customs and attitudes toward Europeans. Remembering the symbolic objects that had served him so effectively during his first mission, Brazzà gave the envoy a rifle cartridge and a French flag, and asked him to have the

Apfourou chief choose between the two. "One is the sign of war without mercy," Brazzà instructed him to say. "The other is a symbol of peace, as profitable to your interests as to ours."

On August 28, 1880, they arrived at Mbé. The envoy set off to confer with the Apfourou chief, while Brazzà and his men were told that King Makoko would receive them right away. The members of the French mission made themselves presentable and produced their best attire to meet the Bateke ruler. Brazzà put on his dress uniform with gold trim, and gave his men a final inspection while Ossiah struck the large double bells outside the palisade that surrounded the royal residence.

The gate opened, and Brazzà and his men entered, his marines carrying their rifles pointing downward, in accordance with the local custom. As they approached the royal reception area, Makoko's subjects spread fine carpets and lion skins in the guests' path. A red canopy hung over the low, cushioned throne that awaited the King. Before it, servants placed an antique European copper platter, where the King would rest his feet. It was said that the Makoko's power was such that any ground he walked on became sterile.

Preceded by his great shaman, the gaunt, dignified King Makoko entered slowly, followed by four pages carrying his red robe, and then by his wives and counselors. All were dressed in ceremonial attire, and Makoko wore a wide metal collar with twelve symbolic markings representing the twelve provinces of his realm. He reclined on a lion skin spread over the cushioned throne, while his wives and children settled in around him.

The great shaman knelt before the King, placing his hands in those of his ruler. Then the shaman rose, and paid the same homage to Brazzà, who was seated on one of the bundles of fabric he had brought as gifts. The young lieutenant was introduced by Ossiah, who then translated the King's message of welcome:

"Makoko is happy to receive the son of the great white chief of the West, whose acts are those of a wise man. The King receives him in consequence, and wishes that when he leaves this land, he can tell those who sent him that Makoko welcomes white men who come to him, not as warriors, but as men of peace."

Mentioned by Portuguese travelers as early as the 15th century, Makoko's dynasty and realm were hundreds of years older than those of Leopold II, King of the Belgians. The Makokos were among the most powerful rulers in west central Africa, where they held not only political authority but also great religious influence over all the tribes of the Bateke nation. The domain of this king, Makoko Eloi I, extended from the Atlantic coast to the right bank of the Congo, from the Pool to the confluence of the Alima, and beyond. He was kept informed of all that transpired in his territory, and had heard much about Brazzà, Stanley, and other European travelers. But until today, Makoko had never met a white man.

The King rarely left his palace. It was believed that if he were to see the Atlantic Ocean or the Congo River, he would lose his magical powers. All he knew of the events in his realm came to him through the words of his subjects, and their stories of the various white visitors had often astounded him. Having heard many reports about Europeans, Makoko well understood the difference between the missionaries, who spoke of a mysterious new god, the traders, who exchanged their goods for ivory and slaves, and the explorers, who were now seeking land of their own in his domain.

These white men were sent by great foreign kings. They offered valuable gifts and weapons, and could provide protection from enemy tribes. Makoko realized that he would eventually have to deal with one of them. But which one?

The King had heard that there was a small white man with a thick mustache and an aggressive demeanor who had made his way by force down the great river. He was a rich man with many soldiers and a huge supply of formidable weapons, including one that made boulders explode. The tribesmen called him *Bula Matari*, or "Breaker of Rocks."

Another white man, tall, calm, soft-spoken, had come from the Atlantic coast through the Ogoway. He had fewer men and fewer weapons, but had been a guest of many tribes and had earned their friendship. Several times he had purchased groups of slaves only to set them free, and these freedmen often referred to the tall white man as their "father." So it was that Makoko had decided to invite Brazzà to his palace at Mbé.

The King seemed impressed by the young lieutenant, but no decisions would be made hastily. Makoko spent a dozen days in parley with his honored guest, asking him many questions about his native land, his family, and his intentions in equatorial Africa. For his part Brazzà enjoyed his conversations with the King, and he appreciated the extremely cordial welcome given to him and his men. The Bateke ruler "would not have treated his own children any better than we were treated," wrote Brazzà. Makoko's queen,

Ngassa, insisted on serving the lieutenant his meals, and nearly everyone in the village brought them gifts.

"While we do not fear war any more than do white men, we prefer peace," confided Makoko one day. "I have consulted the spirit of a great wise man, my fourth ancestor, and... I have resolved to guarantee peace by becoming friends with the white man who is worthy of my trust." As a gesture of alliance, Makoko gave Brazzà a bracelet made of the same metal as the King's ceremonial collar.

If in Belgium the French lieutenant had made an enemy of King Leopold II, here in Africa he had made a powerful friend for life. Throughout the many years Brazzà would spend in Gabon and Congo, Makoko's benevolent presence would accompany and protect him in his dealings with the tribes.

To formalize their agreement, Brazzà proposed a treaty by which Makoko would place his domain under the protection of France, and would cede them some territory on the banks of the Congo to establish a settlement. On September 10, 1880, Makoko called an assembly of all his vassal chiefs. The treaty was read in French and in the local dialect, copied in triplicate, and signed by Brazzà and five of the chiefs. The King, and each of his vassals in turn, sprinkled some earth into a box that the grand shaman presented to the French lieutenant, saying, "Take this earth and bring it to the great chief of the white men. It will remind him that we belong to him."

Brazzà planted the French tricolor flag in front of Makoko's palace. "Here is the sign of friendship and protection that I leave with you. Wherever this emblem of peace waves, France will protect the rights of all those beneath it."

It was time for Brazzà to take leave of the King, and to choose a site near Stanley Pool for the second French station. Before he could do that, however, he needed to establish friendly relations with the Apfourous. Hearing of Brazzà's earlier problems with the fearsome tribe, Makoko asked the Apfourous, his allies, to call an assembly to which the French lieutenant would be invited as the King's personal friend.

Brazzà and his men were guided down the Congo to attend the great council. All forty Apfourou chiefs were in attendance, dressed in their finest ceremonial robes and accompanied by hundreds of their followers. All were silent as Brazzà spoke. "You are aware," he said, "that on our last visit to the Alima, we used our weapons only in self-defense. We could have proceeded further down the river, but by withdrawing in the face of your interdiction, and by living in peace in every village we visited, we gave proof of our good intentions. Today we wish to establish a village in the upper Alima, and another at the Pool, in order to trade European and African goods. A peace agreement would be in the interests of your peoples as well as ours."

There followed a long discussion of trading rights on the river. Then one chief approached Brazzà with a grave, defiant air. "Look at that island," declared the chief. "I feel it is there to warn us against the promises of the white men. For it will always remind us that Apfourou blood was spilled in that place by the first white man we ever saw. Our enemies were able to escape us by fleeing like the wind down the river -- but if they return, they will not escape from us a second time!"

Even though Brazzà had heard about Stanley's violent encounter with the Apfourous, and had been expecting this remonstrance, he was deeply moved by the chief's statement.

It required all the young lieutenant's diplomatic skills to explain that Stanley's actions represented neither Brazzà's homeland, nor his intentions. He assured them that the agreement he sought would assure peace and free trade, and would prevent such deplorable incidents.

The peace agreement was concluded with a symbolic ceremony. A deep hole was dug, into which each chieftain placed a bullet, a flint, some gunpowder, or another object representing war. Brazzà and his men tossed in rifle cartridges. Then a small tree was planted over the ammunition, and the hole filled in with earth, as one chief announced, "We bury war so deeply that neither we nor our children will be able to dig it up, and the tree that grows here will serve as a witness to the alliance of whites and blacks."

"We too bury war," said Brazzà. "May peace last until this tree brings forth bullets, cartridges, and gunpowder."

After a few days of feasting, Brazzà and his men sailed down the Congo to found their settlement. As they traveled south with the current, they saw the great river widen even more, into an immense lake containing many islands. Now the French mission had arrived at its final destination, at the fabled place of the gathering of the waters. The tribesmen called it Ncona; to Europeans, it was "the Pool."

Brazzà chose Ntamo, the last village before the rapids, as the place for the French station. Its slight elevation gave it wide view over the Pool, and its strategic location made it the key to the upper Congo.

It was now October 3, 1880. In the fourteen weeks since the founding of Francheville, Brazzà and his dozen men had covered nearly 500 miles, had concluded a treaty with the most powerful ruler in the land, and were about to establish their second settlement. The tricolor flag was raised over Ntamo, and Malamine, promoted to sergeant for the occasion, was placed in charge with three of his marines. Brazzà began the long journey back to the coast, intending to depart soon for France where he hoped to rest, recover his health, and have his treaty with Makoko ratified by the French government.

Reaching the lower Congo, Brazzà noticed an increasing hostility among the tribesmen, and learned that his party was nearing the camp of another white commander. It was *Bula Matari*, who was blasting his way through the rocky terrain to build a road around the rapids. At last, the French lieutenant would meet Stanley, the famous and formidable explorer!

Stanley had set up his headquarters at Mdambi Mbongo, near the village of Matadi. Having put aside his explorations of new territory, he was now devoting his single-minded energy to carrying out the orders of his new employer, Leopold II, King of the Belgians. Thanks to Leopold's omnipresent spies, Stanley had heard about Brazzà's presence in equatorial Africa, but he considered the Frenchman of little importance. As far as the Anglo-American was concerned, he was not involved in any sort of competition or race to the Congo, and he felt no urgent need to establish a Belgian settlement on its banks. It was he who had discovered and mapped the Congo River, and the fact that he had named the great lake above the rapids "Stanley Pool" was proof enough of his conquest.

Nevertheless, Stanley took Brazzà seriously enough to refer to him as "the Challenger." When on November 7, 1880, he was handed a card with the handwritten words "Pierre Savorgnan de Brazzà," Stanley welcomed the opportunity to meet the man that the Africans called "the other great white chief." He gave his scout orders to bring Brazzà and his men to the camp, and instructed his cook to prepare a meal.

The legendary explorers met for the first time in the shadow of the Mayombe Mountains, at Stanley's comfortable, well-appointed camp. Rarely were two men more different. Brazzà, the tall, dark, and aristocratic Roman, was bearded and a bit unkempt though he wore his dress uniform, cocked hat and, unusually, a pair of shoes. The short, stocky, balding Stanley was cleanshaven, with a well-groomed mustache. He prided himself on being neatly dressed in fresh, crisp clothes and shiny boots even in the African bush.

The men shared a sumptuous meal and exchanged pleasantries despite Brazzà's limited English and Stanley's nonexistent French. Stanley puffed on his pipe, while Brazzà smoked cigarettes. Neither man's account of the meeting mentions the oddity of a rivalry between a Welsh-American conquering Africa for the Belgians, and an Italian claiming territory for the French.

Beyond the language difficulties, their conversation was something of a poker game in which each tried to learn about the other's progress without revealing too much about his own. Using all his diplomatic talent, Brazzà praised his host's achievements and spoke sincerely of his admiration for Stanley's definitive exploration of the Congo and his resolution of the age-old mystery of the African waterways. Stanley seemed pleased, and brought Brazzà to see the current site of his road construction project. At that moment his workers were preparing to dynamite their way around the formidable Ngoma Mountain.

The next morning, after a rare comfortable night's sleep in the luxury of Stanley's camp, Brazzà mentioned that he had established a French station at the Pool, and left it under the control of his Senegalese sergeant and several marines. Immediately he noticed his host's irritation at the news. Stanley was now forced to come to terms with the fact that his Continental guest was more than just an admiring visitor. Despite Stanley's fame and Leopold's fortune, the Belgian expedition would not have free reign in the Congo territory.

Thanking his host for the cordial welcome and the fine meals and accommodation, and giving Stanley most of his medical supplies, Brazzà took his leave and set off with his men toward Libreville. His host swiftly began writing a report of the visit to the Belgian King, requesting more staff to safeguard their territory. "At that time," Stanley would later observe, "... I did not appreciate rightly the position of this gentleman."

Future events would give him reason to change his mind.

CHAPTER EIGHT -- THE TOAST OF PARIS

Arriving in Libreville on December 15, 1880, with a small group of companions, Brazzà assumed that his second mission was completed, and that he would soon be boarding a ship back to France. The young explorer was thoroughly exhausted and emaciated and badly in need of rest. In fact, he had never fully recovered from the bronchitis and liver problems with which he had been diagnosed two years earlier, and once again his legs were covered with infected scrapes and sores.

But disappointing news awaited him in Libreville. Ballay and the steamboats, expected the previous June, had never arrived! Neither had the food or construction supplies, nor the reinforcements to staff the new posts. Had something happened to Noël Ballay? Had the French government not received Brazzà's dispatches, or had they changed their minds about his mission? The French naval station at Libreville had no answers to give him.

There was also a substantial cash flow problem. Upon leaving Europe a year earlier, Brazzà had been advanced only 20,000 francs of the 150,000 franc "credit" that he had been allotted for the mission. His family's generous contribution had enabled him to see to his party's basic needs, but now he was running short of everything and required another advance as soon as possible. Here again, the naval commander at Libreville had nothing to offer.

Try as he might, Brazzà could find no explanations for these delays, and could not help feeling mystified and frustrated. After all, he had carried out his orders to the letter. Just as his superiors had entrusted him to do, he had established good relations with all the local tribes, including the fierce Apfourous, and had negotiated a peace treaty with the most powerful ruler in the region. He had founded two French medical and scientific stations, and left members of his mission to safeguard the new sites, Noguez in Franceville, and Malamine at Ntamo. These men could not continue to wait indefinitely, without supplies or reinforcements. If Brazzà did not receive some official support soon, all his efforts would be wasted.

Weary as he was, Brazzà realized that he had no choice but to replenish the two French stations himself. Twenty-four hours after his arrival in Libreville, he set off again with a larger group of marines and some Gabonese carpenters and other tradesmen, and a substantial amount of food supplies for his staff in the bush. At Lambarene the party met Michaud, whose rowers were threatening mutiny after a six-month wait.

Farther down the Ogoway, Brazzà's pirogue capsized, forcing him to spend hours in the water trying to save his supplies and equipment. He ended the day with a serious case of dysentery and a badly injured left foot. A local shaman treated the bleeding foot with an ointment that caused it to swell up "as large as my leg," noted Brazzà. Having left his medical kit in Stanley's camp, Brazzà had no choice but to use his own knife to cut away the infected flesh.

Reaching Franceville in February, Brazzà had the honor of being the first patient treated at the new hospital station. As he recovered, he was pleased to see that Noguez had maintained excellent relations with the local tribes. A few dwellings and other structures had been built; crops and livestock were prospering, and Franceville was already producing enough food to support its inhabitants.

Brazzà spent the next few months writing letters to government officials in Paris, requesting logistical support for the new settlements, and trying to obtain information on any other decisions that had been made. He heard little in return.

In a long letter to his mother, he explained the reasons for his delayed return, and the desperate state of his finances. Because of his hurried and secretive departure from Liverpool in 1879, he had not even been able to visit his family in Italy before leaving Europe. Assuming he would be back within eight months, he had brought only minimal supplies. Now, after spending fifteen months in equatorial Africa and covering more than a thousand miles, largely on foot, his clothes and shoes were in tatters. Once again, the family fortune would have to come to his aid.

Stanley, meanwhile, was also seeking some answers. Since his conversation with Brazzà in November, he had realized that the French presence at the Pool would have to be taken seriously, and he decided to settle the matter in person. A terrible attack of fever in the spring of 1881 brought the intrepid *Bula Matari* to the brink of death, but as always, he recovered. Leaving the road construction project in the capable hands of a recently-arrived German engineer sent by

Leopold, Stanley marched northeast with a detachment of 70 Zanzibarite troops and arrived at the Pool in late July.

A few hours later Stanley saw a small delegation of soldiers approaching with a French flag. They were led by an officer Stanley described as "a dashing-looking Europeanised negro (as I supposed him to be, though he had a superior type of face), in sailor costume, with the stripes of a non-commissioned officer on his arm. This was Malameen, the Senegalese sergeant left by Monsieur de Brazzà. Two Gaboon Negro sailors, in blue navy shirt and pants, followed him, one of whom carried the flag. Malameen spoke French well, and his greeting was frank and manly."

Sgt. Malamine showed Stanley the letter Brazzà had written leaving the sergeant in command of the French settlement, and a copy of the Makoko treaty with which Malamine was to notify all Europeans that France possessed the rights to the entire shoreline territory within a ten-mile radius of the Pool. Stanley was outraged at the thought that a few documents and a tricolor flag could assure someone else the rights to land he considered his own by virtue of his years of exploration and conquest. Nevertheless, realizing that he was in conflict with France, a major European power, Stanley did not resort to the violent methods he habitually used with his African adversaries. He decided to negotiate, and apart from sending a few scouting parties to harass Malamine from time to time, Stanley kept to his decision.

Taking the diplomatic route that had served Brazzà so well, Stanley visited Gamankano, the local chief, who maintained that King Makoko had no rights over the south bank of the Pool. Several months of discussion ensued, at the end of which Gamankano recognized the theoretical authority of Makoko, while Makoko, viewing *Bula Matari* as a potentially useful ally, granted Stanley the right to establish a Belgian settlement on the southern shore of the Pool. Thus were established the first historic boundaries of the future French and Belgian Congo colonies, now the two Congo Republics of the 21st century. Thus began, also, a lingering "cold war" and rivalry between the two brother lands which endures to this day.

Malamine kept Brazzà informed of the new developments, which Brazzà in turn included in the reports he sent regularly to the French Ministry of the Navy. In August 1881 Brazzà was heartened by the arrival of "reinforcements" in the form of French missionaries. Along with civil and military personnel, Brazzà had requested the establishment of French Catholic missions to strengthen the French presence in the territory. Brazzà himself was more of an atheist than a fervent Catholic, but like most Europeans involved in the colonization of Africa, he saw Christian missionaries, if not as direct emissaries of his government, as representatives of his country's civilization and culture. Brazzà felt that France had many advantages to offer Africa, particularly in the area of individual rights and freedom from slavery. Whether through idealism, misplaced optimism, or naïveté, he did not yet realize that instead of stamping out the plague of slavery, the colonial powers would propagate it into an epidemic.

Like the explorers who preceded them, European missionaries came to Africa for a variety of reasons. In most cases they felt a genuine desire to propagate the word of God, and to do good by establishing clinics and schools, but these laudable aims were often tinged with other motives. Missions were frequently established with political goals in mind, and they received generous subsidies from the colonial powers to maintain a European presence and to provide material support for traders, explorers, and occasional military missions. Their school curricula reinforced European cultural values in mission-educated children.

Because of their close contact with the local populace, missionaries were excellent sources of information on the tribes. They were sometimes asked to mediate in and resolve delicate diplomatic matters between the colonial administration and the tribal chieftains. This complex role made the missionary a key player in the establishment of colonial rule.

Father Prosper Augouard, born in 1852, the same year as Brazzà, was to have an influence nearly as great as that of the naval lieutenant himself on the development of France's Gabon and Congo colonies. A Holy Spirit missionary in Gabon since 1877, Augouard was transferred a few years later to the Congo territory, where he established missions at Landana, Mfoa, and Linzolo.

Energetic, strong-willed, and physically imposing, Father Augouard adapted well to the tropical climate and seemed immune from the ailments that tormented most European residents. Amazed at his constant activity in spite of the debilitating heat and humidity, the tribesman named him *Diata-Diata*, or "Quick-Quick."

When Father Augouard arrived in the area of the Pool, Stanley was the first European he met. The explorer gave the missionary a warm welcome, and the two men found that they had many ideas in common. Augouard, who liked to call himself "the Vicar of the Cannibals," shared Stanley's disdainful attitude towards the Africans and his often brutal pragmatism. Stanley invited the missionary to stay at his camp, telling him that the local Batekes were hostile, and specifically warning him against Malamine and the troublesome Brazzà.

Bearing this advice in mind, Augouard went to visit Brazzà's new settlement at Ntamo, where he could see the French tricolor flag flying. But much to the missionary's surprise and annoyance, the guards refused to let him enter the camp, saying no white man was allowed on the land. The guards knew that Augouard had come from Stanley's camp, and assumed he was a member of the Belgian expedition.

Furthermore, Augouard was not wearing the "sign of recognition" decreed by Brazzà. Before he left, Brazzà had instructed Malamine and the guards to refuse entry to anyone not wearing a feather in his hat. For reasons of his own, Brazzà had chosen not to communicate this information to the French Catholic missionaries.

The proud Father Augouard was not pleased. This contretemps marked the beginning of a long-simmering feud between the French missionaries and Brazzà's nascent administration. Augouard would remain particularly resentful toward Malamine. "I had no small difficulty," he wrote, "in recognising the proud representative of France in this big Negro, scantily clad in native fashion and with his hair in plaits resembling the ribs on a melon, as worn by the most elegant members of the Bateke tribe... He is almost black, quite uneducated, unable either to read or write... He is a simple Senegalese sailor, who hardly seems suited to sustain the honor of the French flag...."

These interpersonal conflicts were mirrored by the increasingly bitter European political rivalry for African colonies, and Brazzà found himself right in the middle of it. His letters to his superiors at this time were sounding more and more imperialistic. To maintain the French government's interest in the Congo territory, Brazzà stressed the abundance and value of the land's natural resources such as ivory, rubber, precious hardwoods, and minerals. Most European exploration and reconnaissance of the land between the Congo River and the coast had been carried out by Frenchmen, he stressed, but the few merchants developing the trade in these valuable commodities were British. Envisioning an equitable partnership with the African tribes which would be profitable to both parties, Brazzà nevertheless emphasized in his writings that if any European partner was to gain from the trade, that partner should be France. "Let us not be simply the police force of modern colonization," he wrote. "Of course we should be humanitarian, but patriotic above all." At age 29, the Roman-born Count of Brazzà had spent only seven years of his life in France, but his vocation as a French naval officer was deeply ingrained in his heart and mind.

Despite his unflinching loyalty to France, Brazzà received only rare and somewhat confusing responses to his appeals for administrative support. In late September, tom-toms announced the arrival of another white man. It was Lt. Louis Mizon, sent to replace Brazzà as head of the mission. Brazzà was being called back to France. Ballay had finally arrived in Libreville, reported the taciturn Mizon, but the steamboats had proved to be defective, and Brazzà's long-planned river transportation scheme might have to be abandoned.

After hearing these minimal bits of news, Brazzà was more mystified than ever. He remembered Mizon, of course, whom he had known a dozen years earlier on the *Borda* as his *fistot*, or a member of the naval academy class a year younger than Brazzà's. But despite his title, Lt. Mizon was no longer a French officer. For reasons unknown to Brazzà, Mizon had left the navy and was now working for the French Committee of King Leopold's International African Association. Besides this official irregularity, Mizon soon proved to be a troubled, irascible individual not particularly suited to command an isolated African post like Franceville. The Gabonese tribesmen soon nicknamed him "Commandant 'Get the hell out of here'" after his most commonly-uttered phrase.

By the fall of 1881 Brazzà's strength had returned. With a short speech stressing that slavery had been abolished in the Ogoway region, and that Franceville would always be a haven for runaway slaves, he transferred control of the mission to Mizon. Making certain that both Franceville and Ntamo had sufficient provisions, Brazzà decided to do a bit more exploring before returning to France. He headed south, tracing the Ogoway to its source, and crossed the Niari-Kouilou basin in search of an easier route from the coast to the Congo River. By April 1882 he was making his way toward Libreville to sail home.

Before boarding a British cargo ship back to Europe, Brazzà retrieved his mail, which included a letter from King Leopold. Apparently the Belgian monarch had been kept fully informed of the French officer's successful negotiations with Makoko, and the achievement had only increased the King's animosity. "Try as he might," wrote Leopold, "Monsieur de Brazzà will never have his treaty ratified. We will play with the Congo territory as if it were a toy. Monsieur de Brazzà would make better use of his time by coming to work for us." First there had been Stanley's challenge to Malamine, then the inauspicious arrival of Mizon, and now this threatening letter addressed directly to Brazzà. At nearly every turn, the young lieutenant seemed to come across another of Leopold's tentacles.

There was more bad news. Mizon had inexplicably recalled Malamine from the strategic French station at Ntamo. The long-awaited steamboats had proved so defective that Ballay had already sailed back to Europe in search of replacements. Worst of all, Noguez had died of fever in Franceville.

Where would all these frustrations end? And what sort of welcome awaited Brazzà in Paris? Doubts and depression haunted his thoughts as he and Michaud sailed back to Europe. When their ship docked at Portsmouth, England in early June 1882, the two ragged French officers had no local currency to their name, and sought the aid of the French consul. Requesting instructions from Paris, the consul received a telegram with this laconic reply: "Pay fare to repatriate Brazzà immediately by cheapest means possible."

Later the same day, the two men arrived at Paris' Gare du Nord railroad station only to be amazed by a hero's welcome right at the train platform, which had been decorated with flags. Brazzà's old friend Montaignac was waiting with a delegation from the Paris Geographical Society, and its president, Ferdinand de Lesseps, made a speech in Brazzà's honor. The young explorer was then brought to the Society's meeting already in progress, where everyone rose to greet him. Heartened by the enthusiastic reception, Brazzà could not help wondering about the reasons behind it.

He soon learned that the French political scene had changed considerably during his absence. The colonial question had evolved from a secondary issue to one of many critical and controversial subjects. One of Brazzà's principal allies, the pro-colonial Prime Minister Jules Ferry, had favored a military campaign in Tunisia that had gained nothing but the ire and jealousy of Britain and Italy. Ferry had also reorganized the French educational system, making primary instruction obligatory even for girls, and establishing free public schools. These innovations had launched a religious war with the Catholic Church, which had previously held a virtual monopoly on primary education. Ferry's opponents on these and other issues became so vociferous that his government had collapsed in November of 1881.

Another of Brazzà's supporters, Gambetta, was trying to win support for a French offensive in Egypt to counter the British advances there. Right-wing deputies maintained that colonial policy was too expensive, while left-wing nationalists were furious that France's military forces were not concentrated on recovering the two lost eastern provinces of Alsace and Lorraine from Germany. Alliances now linked Germany with Russia, Austria-Hungary, and Italy, placing France in an increasingly vulnerable position. At the same time, a few pro-colonial partisans felt that Brazzà's Congo territory could provide France with a tractable and possibly very lucrative colony that would enhance the Republic's international prestige, especially in the face of the burgeoning British Empire. Clamorous debates on all these subjects intensified throughout 1882, and the absence of well-defined political parties in France only added to the confusion.

Brazzà realized that he would need a strategy to make his voice heard above the chaos. Most politicians were too engrossed in their affairs to listen to him, and French businessmen were still skeptical of the viability of investing in central Africa. As for the military establishment, they had always been a bit wary of the charismatic and independent Brazzà.

The young lieutenant sensed that his strongest support would come from the French people. A fascination for the exotic still dominated their favorite books, art, and entertainment, and Brazzà knew that he could excite their enthusiasm with his tales of adventure. The late-19th-century public was particularly eager to hear of patriotic exploits that reinforced their ideal of France as a great civilized and civilizing nation. Brazzà's noble family background and his reputation as a humanitarian, not to mention his attractive looks, made him a natural popular hero.

Brazzà found his most faithful advocates among the scientific and intellectual community, who appreciated the great contribution his missions were making to their knowledge of central African geography, ethnology, fauna, and flora. Although the learned class had little financial backing to offer him, their opinion carried substantial weight with both the public and the government, and the events they organized in his honor were given wide coverage in the French press. The Sorbonne honored the young explorer with a grandiose ceremony attended by Brazzà's mother, the Countess Giacinta, who besides her affectionate letters had sent generous financial contributions to further her son's efforts.

At the Paris Historical Society, the "young and heroic traveler" was praised for beginning "a new chapter in French colonial history," and for opening Africa "to civilization and to France." Brazzà replied with a modest speech praising France's "great and generous ideas," but tactfully omitting the fact that Africa already possessed civilizations of its own, in the form of elaborate societies that he himself had spent years observing.

In reality, Brazzà probably saw little difference between his popularity campaign in Paris and his colorful diplomatic negotiations with Makoko and the other chiefs. In either case, he deftly used whatever charm and props were necessary to obtain the support he needed. His ultimate goal, after all, was an honorable one: not personal gain, but a genuine and meaningful cooperation between his adopted country and the colony he would help create.

The Paris Geographical Society gave him the most enduring tribute of all. At their gala reception, Ferdinand de Lesseps announced that the modest station at Ntamo would thereafter bear the name of Brazzaville. It was a remarkable honor for a 30-year-old lieutenant and naturalized citizen, already the recipient of many of France's most coveted honors. In his subsequent lectures and writings, Brazzà made a point of expressing his gratitude for this great distinction, always noting that the decision to name the city after him had come from the land he served. "I am not the guilty party," he jested.

A few months after being repatriated from England by "the cheapest means possible," Brazzà had become a household name, and France's favorite romantic hero. His social engagements figured prominently in the Parisian press, much to the displeasure of King Leopold II who could not help but hear of the French explorer's increasing popularity. The Belgian monarch decided he would make another attempt to woo Brazzà to his camp.

On September 12, 1882, Brazzà arrived at the Royal Palace in Brussels in answer to the King's invitation. This time the young lieutenant was treated with the utmost courtesy. Leopold increased his offer, but met with the same reply from the loyal Frenchman, who despite his impeccable courtesy barely hid his disdain for the King's "humanitarian associations."

On the heels of Brazzà's rejection of him, Leopold received another piece of unwelcome news: Stanley had returned to Europe earlier than planned. Easily outdistancing Brazzà in terms of miles covered in the African bush, Stanley had few of his challenger's diplomatic skills. Leopold feared, and with good reason, that one of Stanley's blustery outbursts would soon demolish the elaborate cover of the Belgian King's "international civilizing mission," and reveal it as the greedy grab for wealth that it was.

October 1882 found Stanley in Paris as a guest of the Stanley Club, established five years earlier by his supporters in the French capital. *Bula Matari*, the fabled "Breaker of Rocks" who had located Livingstone and crossed the Dark Continent from east to west, had as many admirers in Paris as did Brazzà, and French journalists took pleasure in instigating a rivalry between the two. The press-induced competition between the Anglo-American explorer and the French lieutenant was little more than a continuation of the eternal animosity between Britain and France, recently aggravated by France's definitive loss of authority in Egypt to the British.

Unfortunately, his international reputation as a brave explorer and foreign correspondent had not diminished Stanley's profound feelings of social inferiority. Unlike a 21st-century American who would be proud to have risen to fame from humble beginnings, Stanley was the product of a Victorian society whose class distinctions were as immutable as the bars of an iron cage. In Africa he could fancy himself an all-powerful conqueror, but as soon as he returned to Europe, Stanley was again confronted with the dreaded secrets of his illegitimate birth, workhouse childhood, and improvised education. Pierre Savorgnan de Brazzà, eleven years younger and a foot taller, represented everything that Stanley would never be: a handsome, confident, cultivated nobleman with perfect manners and Mediterranean charm.

Stanley soon became inflamed with jealousy and rage at all the attention his French "challenger" was receiving, and at Brazzà's published remarks that the Anglo-American owed all his progress in Africa to violence and aggression. Brazzà, by contrast, claimed to be a man of peace who traveled as a friend, and was welcomed and respected by the tribesmen. Stanley decided that he would settle the balance at an elegant banquet to be given in his honor at the Continental Hotel, one of Paris' most prestigious establishments, on October 19, 1882.

When the two explorers met by chance on the boulevards earlier that day, Stanley could not resist a verbal thrust at his opponent. "I'm going to have the pleasure of giving you a bit of a mauling tonight," was Stanley's comment, according to his supporters. "I'm going to kill you tonight," was what Brazzà and his French-speaking companions seem to have heard. Taken aback by Stanley's aggressive demeanor, Brazzà did not respond.

The Frenchman had not planned to attend the banquet in honor of his rival, but this incident changed his mind. Returning to his hotel, Brazzà prepared a short speech and had an American student at the Paris Geographical Society translate it into English. Brazzà spent the rest of the afternoon drinking black coffee and memorizing the English text.

Stanley apparently chose to imbibe something much stronger, because that evening he swayed as he approached the podium at the Continental Hotel. Much to the surprise of his audience, he launched into a blustery, boastful speech about his accomplishments in the name of the Belgian king's international humanitarian organization. He described the Congo basin as "a fruitless waste, a desolate and unproductive area" that he intended to "fill with life" and redeem, "to plant and sow that the dark man may gather."

He ridiculed Brazzà, describing the explorer he had met in Africa as "a shoeless, poorly dressed person" in a faded uniform who had covered a paltry amount of territory compared to Stanley's epic treks. Far from being the "apostle of liberty" that he was called in the French press, Brazzà was nothing but a liar and a cheat who had swindled Makoko out of his entire kingdom in exchange for beads, cloth, and a few French flags. Since Brazzà's mission had been financed in part by King Leopold's generosity, what right had he to found settlements for France? This Italian was no French patriot, proclaimed Stanley. He was simply using the French flag "as a cloak to cover a scandalous disregard of moral obligations."

The guest of honor concluded his violent diatribe by cursing any opponent who would stand in the way of the Association's great work, or try to compel Stanley to "abandon Africa to its pristine helplessness and savagery."

Struck silent by the embarrassing tirade, the audience gasped as Brazzà entered the banquet hall. The U. S. Ambassador Levi P. Morton, who was presiding over the event, immediately rose and showed the French lieutenant to a seat at the table of honor, right next to Stanley. Brazzà, calm and cool, requested permission to speak, and began reciting his prepared speech in an English imbued with his Roman accent and charm.

Hearing that Stanley was to be honored in Paris, he said, he was glad of the opportunity to declare publicly that Stanley was in no way his opponent, but his colleague. They were "laborers in the same field." Although they represented different nations, both shared the same goal of progress in Africa. Then, raising his glass, he proposed a toast to "the civilization of Africa by the simultaneous efforts of all nations, each under its own flag."

Reassured by his conciliatory remarks, the audience applauded warmly. They fell silent again when Brazzà turned to Stanley. "I hear that I have been attacked this evening," said the Frenchman. "All I offer in return is this," he said, shaking the red-faced Stanley's hand.

Jubilant at the triumph of Latin diplomacy in the face of Anglo-Saxon aggression, the French morning newspapers heaped praises on Brazzà, who from that day on attained the mythical status of "national explorer" among the French people. Copies of the elegant, exotic portrait photos taken of him by Paul Nadar were on sale everywhere. Merchants began asking to use Brazzà's name and image on a wide variety of products from soap to fountain pens. His favorite dark cigarettes began to be manufactured and sold under the brand label Brazzà, which in turn gave its name to tobacconists' shops and bars all over France.

A month after the banquet, French Foreign Minister Charles Duclerc presented Brazzà's Makoko Treaty to the National Assembly, where it was approved by 441 votes to 3. It was unanimously adopted by the Senate, and became law on November 30, 1882.

3. A photograph of Brazzà taken by Paul Nadar about 1882, at the height of the explorer's popularity in France. Photograph courtesy of the Bibliothèque Nationale de France, Paris.

Brazzà's popularity campaign had succeeded far beyond his expectations, and had crowned his efforts in Africa with official recognition in France. He was promoted to full lieutenant and given the title of General Commissioner for Western Africa. A third mission was approved, with an extensive staff and a much larger budget.

No longer a "barefoot conqueror," Brazzà was now an administrator with considerable responsibilities, and he looked to the future with confidence.

CHAPTER NINE -- THE GENERAL COMMISSIONER

In late autumn 1882, Paris was a thriving metropolis of two million people. Its elegant boutiques and impressive department stores assured its reputation as the world's unrivaled center of fashion. Every evening the Avenue de l'Opéra, the Place de l'Étoile, and other main thoroughfares were illuminated by electric lamps, transforming the capital into the "City of Light."

Business and trade were flourishing, aided by all sorts of technical innovations. The forty-year-old telegraph had been joined recently by the telephone, which brought instantaneous voice communication to Parisian offices. Many bourgeois families were hesitant to install the new invention at home, however. The idea of speaking to any stranger who called, without the least hint of a proper introduction, was a shock to the well-established European system of social contact only within one's familiar circle of friends and acquaintances.

Pierre Savorgnan de Brazzà was now a full-fledged celebrity in Paris. His aristocratic name and familiar face appeared on everything from newspapers to children's games to the omnipresent Brazzà cigarettes. Young Frenchmen began growing beards to imitate his intrepid look. The lieutenant was fêted at one honorific dinner after another. In the last days of December 1882, when his political ally, the gifted statesman and orator Léon Gambetta, died unexpectedly at the age of 44, Brazzà was asked to accompany the funeral cortège. After the ceremony, a cheering crowd carried the young explorer home.

As Brazzà prepared his third mission to the Congo, his most ambitious undertaking to date, letters and propositions of all sorts arrived for him at the Hotel de Bade, his habitual address in Paris' Latin Quarter. Would-be explorers asked to accompany him; young ladies offered their services as wife or housekeeper; people of all sorts shared their tributes, poems, and far-fetched business schemes. Brazzà barely had time to sort through the stacks of mail before returning to his most pressing business, that of recruiting a staff qualified to establish France's Congo Colony.

If Brazzà's current endeavor was backed by considerable financial and logistical support, it was also entrusted with specific political, military, and scientific goals. The mission would set in place the basic administrative infrastructure for the new French colony. It would found more posts to assure the stability of the accords reached with local chieftains, and to guarantee free trade (for the French and their allies, that is) on the Ogoway and Niari-Kouilou river systems.

A fully-equipped naturalist and an assistant would undertake a complete survey of equatorial flora and fauna in the name of Paris' Museum of Natural History. A geographer would accompany the mission to complete Brazzà's already outstanding work in providing detailed topographic maps of the entire region. To carry out these tasks, Brazzà would lead of a staff of more than 200, including 48 Europeans, 25 Algerian sharpshooters, and 130 Senegalese marines.

Much of Brazzà's time in Paris was taken up with banquets, speeches, appointments, and meetings with philanthropists to drum up subsidies. In between the social events, he concentrated on selecting the dozen key officers who would command the various segments of the mission. Noël Ballay and Louis Mizon were already in Africa. Mechanical engineer Joseph Michaud would rejoin the staff, accompanied by his brother Pierre, also a technical specialist. Sergeant Malamine Kemara, currently recuperating in Senegal, would head the large detachment of marines. Brazzà's younger brother Giacomo Savorgnan di Brazzà, who held a doctorate in natural sciences from the University of Rome, would carry out the scientific survey with the aid of his assistant, Attilio Pecile.

François Rigail de Lastours, a civil engineer recently returned from colonial service in Mozambique, shared Brazzà's enthusiasm for Africa as well as his energy. Brazzà hired him to lead the mission's advance party which was set to leave France on January 1, 1883. The gifted writer, linguist, and naval officer Jules-Léon Dutreuil de Rhins, seeking a new challenge after serving in Indochina and Egypt, would be the mission's geographer. Several promising young military academy graduates including Dolisie, Decazes, Manchon, and Fourneau completed the mission's ranks.

The basic elements of the great expedition were now in place. Brazzà's only remaining problem was keeping his head above the overwhelming amounts of paperwork required by the French government. Despite his lingering Italian accent, the lieutenant had no trouble expressing himself in French, having lived and worked in a French-speaking environment since the age of fourteen. But keeping up with the seemingly endless stream of official letters and reports was another matter. He would need an assistant to see to all that.

One afternoon as Brazzà rushed out of his hotel to a meeting at the Ministry of War, a well-mannered young man asked to speak to him. "Yes, what can I do for you?" asked Brazzà hurriedly.

"All I ask is five minutes of your time. My name is Charles de Chavannes. I've come from Lyon, and I've been waiting here in the lobby since nine this morning. I sent you up my card with a note from Dalin, who was a classmate of yours at the Rue des Postes school."

Brazzà's carriage was waiting. "Well, all right. Ride with me to my appointment. We can talk on the way."

Once they were inside the coach, Brazzà continued, "You know, you're the hundredth person to approach me this week. Do you know anything about African exploration? What qualifications do you have?"

"I have a law degree, and I'm a reserve officer in the army. I can do topographical surveys."

"Do you know astronomy? Celestial navigation?"

"No, but I'm sure I could learn anything that is required of me."

They had arrived at the Ministry. Jumping out of the coach, Brazzà called back, "Come and see me tomorrow morning at nine at the Hotel de Bade."

The following morning at nine, the 29-year-old Chavannes was shown into Brazzà's bedroom, where he was greeted by an oddly memorable sight.

"I looked to my left," he wrote years later, describing the scene in his memoirs, "at the metal bed in the corner, and this is what I saw: a long body stretched out under the covers, a head of unkempt brown hair among the pillows, two big, dark eyes still swollen from sleep, and two long arms stretched out on the bed. Next to the bed, an old night table with three or four empty packs of cigarettes and as many boxes of matches, beside a large white chamber pot used as an ash tray."

Brazzà yawned and waved Chavannes to a seat. "Repeat what you told me yesterday."

Chavannes tried to put his best foot forward, and spoke of his law studies and other skills. He belonged to a boating club, and had co-founded the Lyon Rifle Club.

"As I see it," muttered Brazzà, sitting up a bit and leaning on his elbow, "nothing you've told me proves that you have the drive and determination I'm looking for."

Intimidated by the face-to-face meeting with a public figure he so admired, and whose exploits he had followed in the newspapers for years, Chavannes didn't know what else to say. Brazzà promised to keep Chavannes in mind. Who knows, maybe something would turn up, and if it did, he had the young lawyer's address.

Chavannes took the train home to Lyon, thinking back on the unusual yet momentous interview. He was glad, at least, to have met the famous explorer. He hoped against hope for a place in the Congo Mission, but from that point on, all he could do was wait.

Several months passed. In late February 1883, he read that Brazzà's mission was set to depart on March 10th. Well, Chavannes had done his best, and now that he had missed his chance as an explorer, he might as well settle into the quiet life of a provincial attorney.

On March 7th, Chavannes received a telegram as surprising as it was short: "If you can come to Paris, I will be happy to see you. -- Brazzà."

Mystified but hopeful, Chavannes arrived in Paris on the 9th, and called on the explorer immediately. Once again he found Brazzà rushing out to an appointment, and again they rode together in the coach. When Chavannes asked why he had been summoned, Brazzà cried, "Because you're coming with me!"

Chavannes was thrilled. He thanked Brazzà profusely and asked what job he would fill. "You'll be my private secretary," was the response.

"And when should I report for duty?"

"The 12th at Bordeaux. Hotel Richelieu."

That was in three days! "But... I have nothing ready..." stammered Chavannes.

"Go to Conza at 59 rue Meslay, tomorrow. He's our supplier. He'll outfit you with everything you need for the mission." The coach had arrived at its destination, and Brazzà stepped out. "Goodbye," he said. "See you later!"

Excited and breathless, Chavannes could barely believe what he had just heard. He instructed the coachman to take him to Conza, near Paris' Porte Saint Martin. It was a small shop, but plentifully stocked with tropical clothing, mosquito netting, and everything else an explorer might need.

The tailor took Chavannes' measurements, made a note of his name, and immediately began preparing another set of clothing and supplies according to the list Brazzà had established for members of the expedition. One linen suit, one light wool suit, one belt, three flannel shirts. Socks, handkerchiefs, a helmet, a waterproof poncho. Two pairs of hunting boots. It would all be packed, wrapped, and delivered to Bordeaux in time for their departure. Overnight, Chavannes' dream had become reality. The young attorney was now an explorer, on his way to the Dark Continent.

The Congo Mission's advance party had left as scheduled on January 1st, under the command of Rigail de Lastours, accompanied by naturalist Giacomo di Brazzà and his assistant, Attilio Pecile. They would begin the time-consuming process of hiring pirogues, rowers, and porters. In February, Lt. Decazes sailed to Senegal to oversee Sgt. Malamine's recruitment of the marines, while Lt. Manchon set off for Algeria to engage the detachment of sharpshooters and escort them to Libreville. Meanwhile, 350 tons of supplies and provisions were being shipped separately from Liverpool and Hamburg.

On March 19th, Brazzà, Chavannes, and the rest of the expedition departed Paris for Bordeaux. In an address to the Geographical Society of Bordeaux, Brazzà spoke proudly of his new role. No longer the solitary heroic explorer, he was now the leader of a team.

"I need not speak of the past, but of the future. Our work now extends far beyond the efforts of a single man... it is the work of France."

On March 21, 1883, Brazzà's Congo Mission embarked on the three-masted ship *Precursor*. Soon after they had set sail, Chavannes noticed tension and quarrels among some of the staff members on board. He asked Albert Dolisie, an artillery officer, if this was normal behavior. "For a salary of a hundred and fifty francs per month," replied Dolisie, "did you think we were hiring ambassadors?"

Who, in fact, had Brazzà chosen to carry out his idealistic plan of mutually beneficial cooperation between France and equatorial Africa? In the few months he had been given to hire his staff and to accomplish so much else, decisions had been made quickly. Brazzà had relied on intuition and personal references, but above all on the availability of the applicants. Many of the officers he selected, including Chavannes, Dolisie, and Rigail de Lastours, proved to be excellent leaders and devoted friends. As Brazzà's missions grew larger, however, and the colony he helped create required increasingly greater numbers of administrators and functionaries, he necessarily had less and less control over the standards of recruitment.

What motivated the men who sought work in France's colonial service? Some, like Chavannes and even Brazzà himself, were looking for adventure and personal fulfillment. Others hoped for military and professional advancement, which they could obtain much more quickly and easily by serving a tour of duty overseas. Many needed money, and were already fleeing debts in France. A not-inconsiderable number had criminal records. After all, the far-off colonies were a different world, one where Europe's tight social restrictions were rarely enforced. As Stanley knew better than anyone, a white man in Africa automatically possessed a distinctive social status that in most cases would be far beyond his reach in his own country.

In early April the *Precursor* put in at Dakar, where the Congo Mission was joined by 130 Senegalese marines, under the command of Lt. Decazes and Sgt. Malamine. Brazzà was happy to greet the Moorish-Berber sergeant, a dependable colleague and friend whom he had not seen in three years.

Malamine's imposing physical stature and strength were matched by his unwavering discipline and fidelity. Following Brazzà's orders to the letter, Malamine had defended the strategic French post at Ntamo from Stanley's hostile incursions, until the sergeant had been replaced by an officer of Mizon's choosing. In spite of Stanley's belligerence, Mizon's questionable judgement, and King Leopold's ceaseless maneuvering, the French Committee of the International African Association presided over by Ferdinand de Lesseps had transferred control of all the stations Brazzà had founded to the French government. The tricolor flag that Brazzà and Malamine had served so well still waved over the former Ntamo, a growing town that from 1883 was known as Brazzaville.

On April 22nd the Congo Mission arrived at Libreville. From the administrative point of view, little had changed since the early days of the Ogoway Mission in 1875. Brazzà found that no preparations had been made for him at the port, and he and his men were obliged to offload their 800 crates of equipment and supplies for themselves. The French naval station had ignored the order to set aside covered storage space for the Congo Mission's use, and so their enormous pile of costly merchandise had to be left out in the open, subject to pilferage, accident, and the drenching tropical rains. The mission's staff, a number of whom were already ill, had to sleep anywhere they could, since no barracks were available.

Where was the French government's support now? thought Brazzà, as he tallied up the losses incurred in only the first few days. He had had to pay a 2000-franc indemnity to the captain of the *Precursor* for delays in offloading the merchandise. He was losing a hundred times that amount in damage and theft to the supplies, most of which were irreplaceable in Africa. But what point was there in complaining?

The Gabonese tribesmen gave him a much warmer reception. Months earlier they had been pleased to welcome the mission's naturalist, Giacomo Savorgnan di Brazzà, younger brother of the great explorer. Jacques de Brazzà, as he soon became known, ingratiated himself even more by abandoning his boots after the first few days and walking around barefoot. Unlike the straitlaced Stanley, the fearsome *Bula Matari* who earned little more than a grudging respect from the Africans, the Brazzà brothers assured the tribesmen of their sincerity and goodwill by taking off their shoes. In the African view of things, a good-natured, down-to-earth man who showed his feet obviously had nothing to hide.

By May Brazzà was in Lambarene, where he could get updated information from the various outposts and reorganize his plans. He sent out officers to found several new posts and to resupply and take command of the old ones. At the same time, the French navy dispatched a warship to the small Atlantic seaport of Pointe Noire, where King Leopold's armed mercenaries were trying to take control of the French coastal settlement. The increased French military presence, combined with negotiations with the local king, safeguarded Pointe Noire and endowed the French colony with another strategic harbor at Loango on the Atlantic coast.

Brazzà reached Franceville in late July. The first settlement he had founded on the African continent held a special place in his heart, and on returning to this safehaven for runaway slaves, Brazzà was again struck by the beauty of its natural setting. The town's gentle elevation gave him a panoramic view of the surrounding green hills dotted with villages and banana plantations, and of the Ogoway and Mpassa Rivers flowing south and east.

Despite the appeal of its fertile landscape, however, Franceville was beset with problems. Lt. Mizon's brusque treatment of the Gabonese had produced a climate of resentment that required months of Brazzà's patient diplomacy to placate. At the same time, the General Commissioner's work was multiplied by the fact that most of his desperately-needed staff were ill. Franceville's clinic overflowed with patients, largely Europeans who had difficulty adapting to the tropical climate.

A letter from Noël Ballay brought him some good news. After several years of delicate negotiations, the Apfourous had agreed to collaborate with the French in establishing Brazzà's long-dreamed-of riverboat service that would link the coast with the Ogoway, Alima, and Congo waterways. A network of steamboats and pirogues, connected by several portage routes, would provide a safe and dependable way to transport passengers and merchandise throughout the new colony. A station was founded at Diélé on the Alima to serve as the hub of the new enterprise. Brazzà sent Chavannes to aid Ballay in the final negotiations with Mdombi, the Apfourou chieftain.

After training his new administrative staff and supervising the construction of some additional buildings at Franceville, Brazzà joined Ballay and Chavannes at Diélé in September. The young General Commissioner had not seen Ballay for three years, and was glad to find him in good health and to congratulate him on the success of his lengthy diplomatic discussions with Mdombi. The riverboat service was inaugurated with great celebration on October 15, 1883. Four years later, Brazzà noted that although only a minimal surveillance network was in place, the transport system had never suffered a single theft or other incident.

4. Dr. Noël Ballay in 1886. Dr. Ballay accompanied Brazzà on his first mission in 1875. He was later Governor of Gabon, then of French Guinea. Drawing courtesy of the Bibliothèque Nationale de France, Paris.

5. Charles de Chavannes about 1890. Hired as Brazzà's secretary in 1883, Chavannes proved to be a valuable administrator and friend, and a gifted writer. He gave a moving tribute at Brazzà's funeral. Drawing courtesy of the Bibliothèque Nationale de France, Paris.

A huge pirogue with a capacity of eight tons of merchandise was loaded with six months' provisions and supplies, and Ballay and a staff of fourteen men set off up the Alima. The Apfourous' friendship would now allow them to sail serenely past the riverbanks where violent battles had brought Brazzà's first expedition to an abrupt end in 1878.

As Brazzà watched Ballay and his men disappear down the river on their way to the Congo and unexplored regions, a part of the young commander longed to go with them. But as General Commissioner, Brazzà's place was now in the French settlements, assuring their safety and prosperity. The opening of new territories, the first encounters with unfamiliar tribes, the excitement of discovery, would now be left to his younger colleagues.

As Brazzà assumed his less exciting but more responsible administrative role in the French colony, stories of his activities in Africa were undergoing some strange transformations in Europe. Mortified by Brazzà's seemingly unstoppable success, King Leopold was using every possible means to undermine the lieutenant's reputation. Through interviews given by Stanley and his colleagues, and articles written by French journalists in the pay of the Belgian monarch, rumors reported that King Makoko had passed away, that the naturalist Jacques de Brazzà had died of a tropical disease, and that the General Commissioner himself had been murdered by hostile tribesmen.

By November 1883 the Congo Mission's geographer, Jules-Léon Dutreuil de Rhins, had returned to Paris where he spent most of the ensuing winter dispelling the baseless rumors. When on February 1, 1884, a French newspaper reported "the death of the illustrious explorer of the Ogoway, Pierre Savorgnan de Brazzà," Dutreuil de Rhins took the opportunity to give a forceful speech before the Paris Geographical Society. Not content simply to deny the rumors, the geographer alluded directly to their authors. Stanley, the Belgian King's principal explorer, was behind them, stated Dutreuil de Rhins.

"Without manipulating the truth," he continued, "it would be easy to show how desperate Mr. Stanley's situation is at this point. But following Brazzà's instructions to behave correctly at all times toward his rival, I will abstain from commentary."

Stanley had, in fact, lost much of his credibility with the public and with Leopold himself. While presenting a friendly face to Stanley, the King of the Belgians was making arrangements to exclude the intrepid explorer as much as possible from a new colonial master plan that left military exploits behind in favor of sharply increased diplomatic and political maneuvering.

Reports of the recent battle of words in Europe soon traveled to Africa where they went as far as remote villages and colonial settlements. Dufourcq, one of Brazzà's subordinates in Libreville, kept the General Commissioner informed. "The press killed you in October," wrote Dufourcq, "but since you weren't completely dead, they were at it again in January."

But Brazzà was occupied with more important matters. By the spring of 1884 he was establishing new French stations on the Alima on his way to the Congo. At Makoko's royal court, he would present the Bateke ruler with a ratified copy of the treaty they had signed four years earlier. Chavannes accompanied Brazzà on the riverboat that the General Commissioner had named the *Ballay*. As the convoy of ships and pirogues reached the confluence of the two rivers, Chavannes described the startling contrast between the greenish flow of the Alima and the muddy, endless expanse of the Congo.

"Suddenly the rowers stopped their chanting. They held their oars still along the sides of the pirogues... Not a breath of air troubled the immense surface [of the Congo] that looked like a moving mass of molten lead. The air was heavy, and a tepid mist reduced all colors to shades of gray. The strangeness of the sight, and the huge dimensions of the river, made it an intense and sobering experience."

Brazzà, too, was moved by the magnificent view, as he gazed out at the vast river dotted by innumerable tiny islands. Everything was suffused by a misty yellow-gray light in a shimmering panorama.

After a few days on the great river, the convoy came ashore. As they made their way overland to Makoko's palace at Mbé, Brazzà was greeted by many old acquaintances. Each local chief insisted on welcoming him personally. An escort arrived to accompany the Frenchmen to the royal court, where Makoko had arranged a sumptuous ceremony for the return of his greatest white friend.

A small choir sang a song composed in honor of Brazzà's arrival:

> *Truly, truly,*
>   *everyone here can see*
>   *He that they said was dead*
>   *He has returned*
>   *He that they said was poor*
>   *Look at his gifts.*

Following the traditional protocol, Brazzà and the smiling King Makoko took the same number of steps toward each other and embraced. Gifts were exchanged, and the two allies spoke of the four years that had passed since their last encounter. Makoko ordered a meeting of all his vassals to witness the presentation of the ratified treaty.

A few days later, on April 10, 1884, Brazzà, Ballay, Chavannes, Malamine, and their followers were again welcomed to the royal palace. Makoko, carrying a long staff, came to greet them. The King's numerous vassals had gathered beneath a red tent that shaded Makoko's throne. All the chiefs were dressed in brightly-colored ceremonial attire, and most carried statues representing their ancestors.

Makoko and Brazzà shared a cup of palm wine before Makoko reclined on the lion skins laid over his low throne. As always he was surrounded by his wives and children. His vassals, who sat on leopard skins, rose one by one and knelt before Makoko to declare their fidelity to the great King of the Batekes. Then the vassals addressed Brazzà, saying that they were happy and proud to be under the protection of the French flag. They swore their loyalty on the spirits of their ancestors. Brazzà spoke briefly of his friendship with Makoko and the vassal chiefs. The French troops presented arms and saluted the king, as Brazzà solemnly placed before the Bateke ruler the ratified treaty that united his people to those of France.

Brazzà had accomplished his two greatest goals: he had negotiated a treaty with equatorial Africa's most powerful ruler, and he had seen the accord ratified by the French government. Both sides were in agreement, and yet this was still not enough. The territories ceded to the French by Makoko were constantly subject to attack and harassment by other European powers, particularly Belgium. Another agreement was needed, under an international authority capable of enforcing the law in the face of Europe's increasingly violent "Scramble for Africa."

Realizing the need for international regulation of their African colonies, the European powers scheduled the "West Africa Conference" to begin in Berlin on November 15, 1884. Delegations from the United States and from thirteen European kingdoms, empires, and republics, gathered for the meeting which would settle the fate of equatorial Africa. Not a single African was invited to attend.

The conference was hosted by Prince Otto von Bismarck. As Prime Minister of the King of Prussia, Bismarck had orchestrated the humiliating defeat of the French Army in 1870, but in 1884 he welcomed his guests with a polite speech in French. The aim of the conference, he said, was to promote the civilization of the African natives by opening the interior of the continent to commerce. He spoke of the late Dr. Livingstone's fervent wish to bring the "three C's" -- commerce, Christianity, and civilization -- to the Dark Continent.

In reality, the conference was limited to Europe's political and economic objectives. Boundaries, acquisition of new territory, and free trade were discussed in great detail for more than three months. The French delegation included Dr. Noël Ballay, who had brought documents certifying French possession of the territories Brazzà had negotiated with Makoko in the Gabon and Congo regions. Rights to the banks of the Congo River were disputed by at least three nations at the conference: by France, Belgium, and even Portugal, whose claim was based on the travels of 15th-century Portuguese explorers.

On February 26, 1885, negotiations and deliberations were concluded and the General Act of Berlin was signed. The document had little effect on the political and economic organization of Europe's African colonies, but it settled several strategic boundary disputes. Central Africa was no longer a vast, unknown wilderness where bold adventurers vied to plant their country's flags. Brazzà's French Congo, as well as Leopold's Congo Free State, now had a legitimate political existence and could be run by colonial administrators.

The Berlin Conference had two immediate and rather contradictory effects on the lives and careers of Europe's great explorers. In one sense, the new legal status with which the conference had endowed the African territories validated the work of men like Brazzà and Stanley, by turning their conquests into colonies. In another sense, it made the profession of "explorer of Africa" obsolete.

As of 1885, Henry Morton Stanley's days of conquest were over. Apart from an ill-conceived and disastrous diplomatic mission to East Africa in the late 1880s, Stanley spent the rest of his life in Europe.

Pierre Savorgnan de Brazzà would decide differently.

CHAPTER TEN -- THE DIPLOMAT

On July 15, 1885, Brazzà received instructions to return to France. With the official birth of French Congo, his third mission had accomplished its goals and no longer had any reason to exist.

In many ways he was glad to transfer his authority to Commandant Pradier, the new colonial chief, because the past two years had been difficult and costly. Fever and other tropical diseases had taken the lives of several of Brazzà's best officers, including his friend François Rigail de Lastours. Malamine was suffering from exhaustion and was being repatriated to Senegal with a view towards an early retirement. Brazzà himself was again emaciated and weak, and at times had to be carried in a hammock as he made his way to the coast.

Brazzà and Chavannes embarked on the *Albatross* in mid-October for the Portuguese island of Sao Tomé, where they boarded a ship for Lisbon. In Portugal, a misunderstanding resulted in Brazzà's being quarantined for a suspected case of cholera. Resolving the problem through diplomatic intervention, they continued on by train to Madrid and Bordeaux.

Brazzà arrived at Paris' Gare d'Orleans railroad station on November 10th, where he was welcomed by a small but distinguished group of statesmen, intellectuals, and explorers, including Dutreuil de Rhins. Not yet 34 years old, Brazzà appeared thin, tired, and older than his years, but according to a contemporary newspaper report he had not lost the sparkle in his eyes, nor the energy in his voice and step.

The French political scene was still in a state of confusion. Not unexpectedly, many politicians were dissatisfied with the results of the Berlin Conference. Some felt that France's African colonies were a valuable source of prestige and revenue, and that the conference had handed over potentially lucrative French territory to Belgium and Britain. Others thought that the colonial enterprise was a waste of resources and manpower, and that it should be abandoned in favor of a more concerted effort to recover the former French provinces of Alsace and Lorraine from Germany.

Brazzà was criticized as well. Officials inured to their well-established bureaucratic routines in Paris maintained that Brazzà's administrative methods were vague and imprecise, and that his decisions were based more on his own intuition than on proper government procedures. On site in Africa, staff members and missionaries had complained that the General Commissioner never had time to meet with them. Even Ballay and Dolisie, two of Brazzà's most faithful colleagues, felt that he was losing his sense of the mission, and that his judgement was less clear and his orders less flexible than they had been in the early days.

Nevertheless, in the face of all the problems and the heavy personal losses, the results were still overwhelmingly positive: more than 20 French posts had been founded in the Congo, Ogoway, and Niari-Kouilou valleys. Under Chavannes' guidance, the strategically-located town of Brazzaville was flourishing. Rivers had been explored; trails had been cleared; accurate maps had been drawn. Hundreds of specimens of previously unknown species of plants, animals, and fish had been gathered for Paris' Museum of Natural History. Through his patient diplomacy, Brazzà had established friendly relations with many African tribes. The Congo Colony he had created in the name of France totaled over 400,000 square miles and was already yielding 14 million francs per year. More than this amount, however, was being invested back into the colony by France in salaries and infrastructure.

Pierre Savorgnan de Brazzà was still a well-known public figure in Paris, and he had recently been promoted from Knight to Officer in the French Legion of Honor. At his young age he could look back with pride on a long list of achievements. But what was his next move? As he traveled to Rome in December 1885 to visit his family, he finally had the time to do some serious thinking about his future.

Brazzà found himself at a crossroads, both professionally and personally. He would never again be the young explorer at the head of a small, virtually independent mission as he had been ten years earlier. The political situation had changed, and so had he. While he still believed wholeheartedly in the projects he had begun, the unbridled optimism of his youth had been tempered by many difficult experiences. His health had suffered as well. If he returned to Africa, it would be in a more sedentary job, as an administrator or colonial governor.

If he chose, of course, he could remain in Europe and begin leading a more traditional life. He could marry and raise a family. As a naval officer he could request an assignment closer to home, or seek his fortune in another overseas colony as had Alfred Marche, who had just returned to France after five years in the Philippines.

But despite the frustrations, the health problems, the official ingratitude, and the large amount of his family fortune used to augment his missions' insufficient budgets, there was really only one choice for Brazzà. He would keep faith with the French navy and with Africa. After years spent exploring the exotic continent that had always been his dream, he felt a bond to the new colony. His hard-won friendships with Makoko and the other chiefs meant much to him. Who else but Brazzà could maintain the delicate balance between the Europeans and the tribesmen, and insure that the principles of his peaceful philosophy were followed? As for the inevitable administrative duties, if Brazzà did not relish the thought of an office job in Brazzaville or Franceville, he certainly did not belong behind a desk in Paris.

He hoped that a personal life and a family of his own would come in time. Brazzà still received a number of letters from prospective fiancées, but so far he had not met his ideal woman. Perhaps he would meet her soon.

After spending the holidays with his family in Italy, Brazzà was back in Paris in January 1886. He soon realized that if he was to return to Africa as he intended, there were several obstacles to overcome, and as things stood he had little political support. His ally Léon Gambetta had died at the end of 1882. Brazzà's steadfast supporter Jules Ferry, after regaining power in 1883, had suffered another political downfall. Spearheading the effort for a colonial empire to rival Great Britain's, Ferry had pressed for increased investment and presence in France's Indochinese colony, but in the military campaign to wrest Tonkin from China, the French forces had suffered a heavy defeat at Lang Son. Ridiculed in the press as "Tonkin-Ferry," Brazzà's ally had been forced to step down as head of the Council of Ministers.

Politicians were losing interest in the administration, regulation, and development of the colonies, and their apathy was encouraged by certain well-placed members of the business community. Ambitious financiers and speculators, seeing the riches pouring out of the Belgian King's unregulated "Congo Free State," demanded similar concessions in French Congo. Why the delay? they asked. For ten years France had invested large amounts of public money to send military officers and scientists to the Congo Colony. Now was the time to reap the benefits.

Tracts like M. A. Lancher's *Les Richesses africaines et les moyens de les acquérir* ("Africa's Riches and How to Acquire Them") spoke of the great economic potential of the Dark Continent's natural resources, and of its supposedly primitive and submissive work force. The speculators were convinced that Brazzà, with his resolute philosophy of gradual, peaceful development and respect for the tribesmen and their customs, was standing in the way of their colossal profits.

Brazzà met with a cool reception at the various government offices, including the Ministry of the Navy, where it was rumored that his brilliant but highly unorthodox career was nearing its end. After a decade of dealing with the French bureaucracy, however, Brazzà was accustomed to these currents of envy and intrigue. He did not let them undermine his confidence or affect his plans. Even if, as he had heard, King Leopold had purchased the loyalty of influential people at the ministries, in the press, and in the business community, Brazzà knew where his most faithful support was to be found: among the intellectual elite, and with the French people.

Once again Brazzà began making the rounds of Parisian society. He attended banquets and spoke at high-profile events that were faithfully reported in the daily press. The exciting stories of his first three missions of African exploration were being serialized in popular weekly newspapers like the *Journal des Voyages*. Ferdinand de Lesseps, president of the Paris Geographical Society, asked Brazzà to address a special session of the Society which would be open to the public and held in the large Cirque d'Hiver, an auditorium where circus performances and other festive events were held during the winter. This speech would be of critical importance in Brazzà's public relations campaign to renew his mission to Congo. The address was composed by Charles de Chavannes from Brazzà's outline.

On January 21, 1886, before an enthusiastic audience of 5000, Brazzà approached the podium beneath the brightly-painted, tent-like ceiling of the Cirque d'Hiver. Every seat was filled, and the Parisian spectators cheered at the sight of the legendary explorer. Brazzà spoke of his passionate interest in the Congo, and of all that the exotic land had to offer -- a wealth of possibilities not only material, but social, cultural, scientific, and humanitarian. His labors and those of many of his comrades, a number of whom had given their lives for Africa, were only just beginning to bear fruit. It would be foolish, he said, to abandon France's great undertaking at this early stage.

He spoke of the progress that had been made: the settlements, the hospital stations, the many geographic and scientific discoveries, and the treaties made possible by Brazzà's warm friendships with the African chiefs. The most significant advance of all, however, was the economic suppression of the slave trade. Twelve years earlier, the Ogoway Valley's only source of outside income was the sale of slaves, which yielded about 2 million francs per year. By the end of 1885, the slave trade had been replaced by legitimate commerce totaling 14 million francs.

Brazzà and his staff had accomplished all this by adhering to a policy of diplomacy and peace. Using violence to impose France's regulations and customs on Africa's people, he continued, would lead only to failure. A colony should be created without forcing its growth, without inducing it to conform to a preconceived pattern or mold. Businessmen seeking only quick profits, he said, should beware.

"The greatest danger," Brazzà warned, "is that of undoing ten years' work in a single day, because the use of force in a project undertaken with patience and kindness can destroy everything in one blow."

There was much more to be accomplished in the colony, Brazzà added. Long-range planning was needed to insure a detailed technical study of the territory, and to begin the construction of transportation and communication systems that would make further development possible. The task would not be easy, said Brazzà, but the potential rewards were great.

Mentioning the names of more than a dozen of his most effective colleagues, Brazzà stressed that long-term professional relationships were the key to success in Africa. The tribes he had befriended based their allegiance to the

French flag on their respect for those who carried it. "Most often," he said, "their idea of a far-away land is personified by the few of its citizens that they have come to know."

For that reason Brazzà requested that, insofar as it was possible, the French government's projects should continue to be carried out by the same representatives of France, working in the same way with the same tribes. That was the surest way to maintain the hard-won confidence and trust of the African tribesmen. With a thought for Sgt. Malamine, who would long wait in vain for his retirement pension, Brazzà noted that commitments made to African servicemen and functionaries with regard to employment benefits had to be fulfilled expediently and fairly.

The lieutenant reemphasized his confidence in his colonial staff and expressed his gratitude for France's confidence in him. "It will be the honor of my life," Brazzà concluded, "if France adopts my plan as its own."

The speech was greeted with thunderous applause. More than his accomplishments and his enlightened views, it was Brazzà's personality and charisma that won over the Parisian audience just as they had charmed Makoko, the Bateke ruler.

In the midst of the standing ovation, Ferdinand de Lesseps came to the podium to conclude the special session of the Paris Geographical Society. In his closing remarks, he requested that the French government change nothing in the administration of the Congo, and that Monsieur de Brazzà be sent back soon "as governor of our colony."

The next morning's newspapers echoed Brazzà's triumph, summarizing his remarks and describing the audience's enthusiastic response. Their applause was "a signal, practically an order for the French government" to renew Brazzà's mandate. Entrusting Brazzà with the governorship of "this new African France" (as the colonies were commonly called) would be carrying out not only Brazzà's wishes, affirmed an article in *La Patrie*, but those of the French people. Ferdinand de Lesseps later confided to Chavannes, "With all this public support, his way is clear. The government will refuse him nothing."

Brazzà's enemies were not pleased at his success, and they continued to harass him whenever they could. The lieutenant's apartment on the rue Saint Florentin, around the corner from the Ministry of the Navy, had been searched and an important file had been taken. Some editorialists claimed that documents dangerously favorable to Congolese interests had been found.

Brazzà's superiors began requiring that he obtain the navy's authorization for travel of any kind. If he gave a speech or lecture, he was obliged to submit the text to the Ministry beforehand, for official approval. One evening at a banquet given by a learned society in honor of Charles-Marie Le Myre de Vilers, the new French governor of Madagascar, Brazzà was asked to propose a toast, and he did. The next day he received a harsh letter signed by Vice-Admiral Aubé, Minister of the Navy and Colonies, accusing him of having "forgotten that his first and foremost duty" as a lieutenant was to respect military discipline and regulations, and threatening severe punishment if the "first warning was not sufficient."

But only months later, Brazzà's perseverance was rewarded. The Chambers of Commerce joined the French public in supporting Brazzà's endeavor, and by April the Ministry of the Navy had granted him a fourth mission. Brazzà had even succeeded in setting several conditions.

Gabon, an older French possession, and Congo and Ubangi-Shari, relatively new territories, would be administered separately, as three distinct sectors of the colony of French Congo. Brazzà would be allowed to make a wider range of decisions on his own authority, without having to wait months or years for approval from Paris.

As for the flattering title of Governor, Brazzà had rejected it, and with it the notion of being chained to a desk, an office, and a mountain of paperwork. He would remain General Commissioner, a pleasantly ambiguous term that gave him the freedom to move around the territory as he saw fit, establishing his headquarters at Brazzaville, Franceville, Libreville, or wherever he was needed.

On April 17, 1886, a proposal signed (just as the disciplinary note had been) by Vice-Admiral Aubé, Minister of the Navy and Colonies, requested the President's approval for Brazzà's nomination as General Commissioner. The name of the "eminent explorer," read the proposal, was "now inseparable from that of French Congo." Brazzà was hereby empowered to "develop France's peaceful influence" and to "establish sustained commercial relations between formerly mysterious lands" and the coastal stations.

Approved immediately by the President, the nomination was decreed the same day. Pierre Savorgnan de Brazzà was General Commissioner for French Congo, a title he would retain for more than a decade.

CHAPTER ELEVEN -- ROCAMAMBO

Since the conclusion of the Berlin Conference in February 1885, the European powers' Scramble for Africa had begun in earnest. The race by statesmen and diplomats to obtain African colonies was fueled more by political than economic motives, and the effort was largely financed by the taxes of European citizens and subjects who knew little of their countries' far-flung possessions, or how they were governed.

Britain's formidable navy and worldwide empire placed her at the head of the expansionist trend. In 1886, the British were devoting their attention to eastern and southern Africa, where they hoped to establish an uninterrupted belt of colonies from Cairo to Capetown. For their part, the French dominated the north and west African coasts. Germany, Portugal, and Italy sought their own African colonies in Cameroon, Angola, Mozambique, Abyssinia, etc. In the center of the continent, the newly-established Congo Free State was neither an independent state nor a Belgian colony, but rather the private property of King Leopold II.

While the balance sheet of his huge expenditures and meager profits in the Congo Free State would nearly bankrupt Leopold, the permissive and corrupt administration of the territory was very advantageous to European traders, whose dubious business practices yielded sizeable gains on ivory, rubber, and other tropical products. The Europeans' superior weaponry had established an economy based on slavery and violent exploitation of the Africans.

The tribesmen's wives and children were often held hostage until the requisite amount of rubber or ivory was turned over for their release. Failure to produce enough raw materials resulted in torture, amputation of limbs, or execution. Shocking human rights abuses in Leopold's colony were witnessed by missionaries and travelers such as Joseph Conrad, whose experiences in the Congo Free State in 1890 inspired "the horror" of his novella *Heart of Darkness*, published in 1902. In his *Last Essays*, Conrad wrote that his idealized image of Africa had been shattered forever by "the distasteful knowledge of the vilest scramble for loot that ever disfigured the history of human conscience and geographical exploration."

While reports of violence and corruption in the African colonies, often written by missionaries, slowly made their way into European newspapers, French profiteers incited by the example and influence of the Belgian monarch exerted more and more pressure on Brazzà to allow similarly abusive practices in the French Congo. When the General Commissioner refused the traders' demands for business concessions, a stream of articles and editorials critical of him began appearing in the French press.

Brazzà knew that the only way to combat these attacks and to safeguard the colonies from exploitation was to establish lucrative sources of legitimate trade. Delegating the day-to-day administration of Gabon to Ballay, and that of Congo to Chavannes, Brazzà spent 1886 in Europe trying to build the foundations of a viable economic infrastructure for the colonies in commerce, agriculture, transportation, and communication.

Meeting with industrialists and craftsmen in chambers of commerce all over France, Brazzà made an effort to convince them that legitimate investments and business dealings in Africa could produce long-term profits. He found them skeptical. They persisted in viewing the colonies not as attractive potential markets, but simply as a dumping ground for products that were unmarketable in Europe. Brazzà countered that most products on sale in Africa were British, and that the French were disbursing money to establish a political administration in their colonies while merchants from other countries were making considerable gains from a variety of profitable, and legal, business opportunities.

In Rouen, where the French navy's suppliers were located, Brazzà spoke with cotton manufacturers about producing fabric more suited to the African market, and packaging it in bundles that could be carried by porters on their backs. When he was invited to address the Geographical Societies of Le Havre and Marseilles, he approached shipbuilders in these two cities about designing vessels suited to travel on rivers broken by rapids. He also stressed the importance of a regular shipping line between France and her new colonies. Why should the French colonial administration in Gabon and Congo continue to have essential goods shipped from Britain and Portugal? he asked. Brazzà's proposal of a new line from France to Libreville met with such enthusiasm that shippers in Le Havre and Marseilles began fighting over the contract.

Eventually it was decided that the two cities would alternate as starting points for the new route.

In the French capital, Brazzà was still a highly popular figure. In the spring of 1886 Paris' wax museum, the Musée Grevin, began featuring an African scene showing France's "national explorer" in parley with tribal chieftains. For two weeks in July, the Museum of Natural History presented an exhibition of the eighty trunks of specimens collected in equatorial Africa by the Congo Mission's two naturalists, Jacques de Brazzà and Attilio Pecile, along with cultural artifacts provided by Chavannes, Dolisie, and others. The exhibit was reviewed in the scientific and popular press, and nearly 30,000 people came to see the exotic plants, animals, and minerals from France's mysterious new territory located between the Niari and Ubangi Rivers. One of the newly-discovered primates, *Cercopithecus neglectus*, was named for the great explorer and is known in English as "DeBrazza's Monkey."

The General Commissioner returned to Libreville in March 1887, after an absence of eighteen months. As in Paris, he had become something of a mythic figure in the colony. Brazzà was referred to by everyone not as *le commissaire général* but as *le grand commandant*. In tribal dialects this title became *"Rocamambo."*

He began a trip around the colony and was displeased by what he saw. The burgeoning number of European functionaries and merchants were mistreating and starving the tribesmen, who were disappearing back into the forest and refusing to cooperate with the colonial administration. There were also many violent intertribal conflicts. "People are mistreated, abandoned, dead, murdered, and underpaid," Brazzà wrote to Chavannes after his inspection of the Niari-

Kouilou region. "We are going to have to begin everything again slowly..."

But Brazzà found it hard to control his anger and frustration. Quarrels and rivalries seemed to dominate every transaction, be it among the tribesmen, between the French and the Africans, or even among colonial administrators. Noël Ballay was increasingly dissatisfied with Brazzà's management of Gabon, and requested a transfer. Chavannes tried to mediate and reconcile the two. Brazzà felt exhausted and demoralized by the avalanche of problems. After spending more than a year in Europe trying to secure promising business contracts for the colony's future, he had not expected to return to chaos and conflict.

Beyond the internal issues, there were border disputes. Leopold's colonists persisted in trying to establish settlements in France's northern Congo territory, until an international agreement signed in April 1887 forbade the Congo Free State from setting foot on the right bank of the Ubangi River. Germany was advancing toward Cameroon, a valuable and strategically-located land that had become a bone of contention between French, British, and German interests. Brazzà was convinced that the best way to insure the safety of Gabon and Congo was to colonize Cameroon and Chad, as first steps in an eventual link with France's North and West African territories. A French presence in Sudan, as he had proposed to the Ministry of Foreign Affairs in Paris, would bring France's African colonies in contact with the Nile, thereby enclosing several important trans-Saharan caravan routes in an entirely French area. Like most of his contemporaries, Brazzà had come to view the African continent as Europe's giant chessboard.

In the last half of 1887, Brazzà and his colonial administration were frequently discussed in the press. A campaign orchestrated by King Leopold produced a series of articles in French and Belgian newspapers, notably the Brussels-based *Mouvement géographique*, attacking Brazzà and accusing him of mismanagement and financial incapacity. Other newspapers, such as Paris' *Journal des débats*, praised his achievements. Each of the many factions that made up France's political landscape had its own opinions on the colonial question. But most French citizens still had only a vague idea of where the colonies were, how much money was being poured into them, and why it was so important to keep them. European newspapers and political tracts were the average person's only sources of information on the subject. Very few Frenchmen had ever seen, let alone spoken to, an African tribesman.

Brazzà's respiratory and liver problems had begun to trouble him. He requested and received an authorization to recuperate in Europe, and was back in Paris in February 1888. Once again he visited ministries and government offices, and again he encountered the eternal bureaucratic difficulties, but Brazzà no longer had the patience to tolerate, placate and convince people. The past few years' efforts, it seemed, were taking him nowhere. He went so far as to compose a letter of resignation to the Ministry of the Navy, but never sent it.

Already in a weakened state, Brazzà received word that his brother Jacques, by then an acclaimed naturalist and explorer, had died of scarlet fever at age 29, soon after returning to Rome to visit his fiancée. It was another difficult blow. Brazzà's own health was not improving, and his doctors insisted that he put aside all business concerns and take a complete rest. He traveled to Italy for a long visit with his family.

At 36, Brazzà was aware of a void in his life. The loss of his beloved younger brother Jacques had made that even clearer. For more than twenty years, since his arrival at Paris' Rue des Postes School at age 14, Pierre's existence had revolved around his naval career. Despite all the difficulties, he was proud of his accomplishments as an explorer and administrator, but now he needed something more.

Brazzà had never been a religious man and was not to become one, but in June 1888 he joined statesman Jules Ferry and Statue of Liberty sculptor Frédéric Bartholdi in the discipline of Freemasonry. Was he in search of personal, professional, or spiritual support? The answer remains a mystery, as he never discussed the subject in any of his writings. After his initial rapid advancement from the rank of apprentice to companion and then to master in little more than a month, Brazzà's participation in the lodge was minimal. He would resign from Freemasonry in 1904 in protest of the *Affaire des fiches*, a scandal involving secret files kept on military officers in the wake of the *Affaire Dreyfus*. Brazzà's vocation as General Commissioner for French Congo remained the only constant in his life.

In October 1888, Chavannes met Brazzà in Paris and cheered him with the news that things seemed to be taking a turn for the better in the Congo. Brazzà's health had improved and he began planning a return to the colony, where he hoped to take part in the exploration of Cameroon and the Upper Ubangi.

The General Commissioner was also examining the possibility of a rail link between Brazzaville, on the Congo River, and Loango, on the Atlantic coast. As Brazzà explained to French politicians and railroad officials in Paris, the French colony was currently obliged to transport all its goods and personnel on the Congo Free State's railway between Leopoldville and Matadi, the line that Stanley had helped build several years earlier. A new rail line of its own would assure the French Congo's security and self-sufficiency. When Brazzà sailed for the colony in May 1889, he was accompanied by a French railroad engineer who would trace the 300-mile route of the Congo-Ocean Railway, eventually completed at great human and financial cost in 1934.

Deaths, illnesses, and other difficulties brought frequent changes in the colony's staff. Devoted, intelligent, but headstrong, Noël Ballay had received his transfer and was facing a new challenge in West Africa as Governor of French Guinea. In March 1889 Charles de Chavannes, dependable, highly competent, and infinitely more even-tempered than either Brazzà or Ballay, had been named Lieutenant-Governor of both French Congo and Gabon. Because of Brazzà's frequent absences, Chavannes presided over most aspects of the colonies' day-to-day administration.

As did the General Commissioner, Chavannes faced constant pressure to grant commercial concessions to unscrupulous traders. Despite the merchants' frequent reiteration of the widely-accepted notion that a colony existed only to produce tangible benefits for the European power to which it belonged, regardless of the interests of the native population, Chavannes stood his ground. Only fully legitimate businesses that agreed to the ethical standards established by Brazzà, such as humane treatment, fair pay, and a grievance process for African employees, were granted concessions to operate in the colony.

6. Brazzà, seated, meets with an African tribal chief around 1890. Photograph courtesy of the Bibliothèque Nationale de France, Paris.

Of course, each refusal provoked a complaint to the Ministry of Colonies in Paris that Brazzà and Chavannes were favoring local over French interests, and that their administration was standing in the way of the colony's economic development. Criticism mounted to the point that Brazzà's support in the French government was eroding dangerously. By October 1889 he had returned to Paris to plead the case for his equitable methods.

Brazzà needed all the public support he could garner, and over the winter of 1889-1890, he was a frequent guest at Parisian social events. Despite his recurrent health problems, France's 38-year-old "national explorer" was still an attractive and heroic figure, and despite his dwindling bank balance, the Roman-born Count of Brazzà remained the quintessential eligible bachelor to the numerous ladies who admired him from a distance. Among the many people to whom he was introduced that winter, he barely remembered the 29-year-old Countess Thérèse de Chambrun, a popular, independent young lady and member of one of France's most distinguished families. But Thérèse certainly remembered meeting Pierre Savorgnan de Brazzà, and she decided to refuse all her hopeful suitors until the day she would meet him again.

Discouraged by the French government's lack of support for him and for the colony's pressing needs, Brazzà left Paris on April 7, 1890. His friend and colleague Albert Dolisie saw him off at the Gare de Lyon train station. "You had a heavy heart last night, Commandant, as you left Paris, and your suffering saddened me," wrote Dolisie the following day. "In fact for several days, regardless of the efforts you made, you looked dejected... I send you all my wishes for a good trip and good health. I hope your plans succeed, and that you are left in peace...."

Brazzà spent the next five years in equatorial Africa, by turns justifying his expenditures, all of which were now under close scrutiny by the Ministries in Paris, and overseeing the management of the colony while Chavannes recuperated periodically in France. But Brazzà devoted as much time as he could to doing what he loved best, visiting remote sites in newly-explored corners of the territory. The upper Sangha and Ubangi-Shari regions were still subject to incursions by the Germans, British, and Belgians. Brazzà organized and led military campaigns that succeeded in pushing them back.

He also visited the older settlements where he paid calls on Makoko and the other chieftains, who had long since become good friends. As always, Brazzà was warmly welcomed by the tribes, and songs were composed and sung to celebrate Rocamambo's return. The chants praised his fidelity to Africa and declared his superiority to the "evil white man" *Bula Matari*, who by 1890 had definitively returned to Britain.

Along with traditional gifts for the tribal chiefs, Brazzà brought coffee and cocoa plants from the nursery in Libreville, as part of his project to diversify the colony's agriculture by introducing new and profitable crops for export. Despite the budget deficits, French Congo seemed to have achieved a certain level of prosperity. In 1892, when French naval officer Alfred Le Châtelier arrived in Libreville to carry out a confidential inspection mission thinly disguised as a "vacation," Chavannes was so obliging and cooperative in answering his questions, showing him files and organizing his visits to other posts that the inspector was completely won over. Le Châtelier returned to France promising to request more support for Brazzà's projects, such as the rail line. The inspector subsequently managed to gain the French government's approval for a transportation subsidy, but three decades would pass before work was begun on the Congo-Ocean Railway.

In late September 1894, as Brazzà sailed down the turbulent Sangha River aboard the steamship *Courbet*, the vessel crashed against the rocks near the village of Tchoumbiri. Ten passengers drowned, trapped beneath the surface by the weight of the sinking ship. Official papers, files, and photographs were lost, as well as 8,000 French francs destined for the colony's depleted budget. Brazzà managed to swim to safety, but was rescued in such an exhausted state that he was sent to a hospital in Libreville to recover. In January 1895 it was decided that he needed to recuperate fully in France, but to avoid a drastic change of climate, Brazzà traveled to Algeria for a few months to wait until springtime. During the recovery period, he had some time to catch up on his mail.

In Paris, the young Countess Thérèse de Chambrun had not forgotten Brazzà. On the contrary, she had spent the last five years asking her numerous friends and relations for news of the famous explorer. Through her uncle François de Corcelle, France's ambassador to the Vatican, she met several acquaintances of the Savorgnan di Brazzà family, and by 1893 Thérèse had become friends with the elderly wife of Antoine d'Abbadie, a noted scientist and explorer of Ethiopia. Monsieur and Madame d'Abbadie had known Brazzà for fifteen years, and corresponded regularly with him.

The childless Madame d'Abbadie threw herself wholeheartedly into the matchmaking process. By late 1894, she had been mentioning Thérèse in her letters to Brazzà for more than a year, but it was only during his convalescence that the General Commissioner found time to respond. He showed interest in the plan, and wrote that he was happy to find himself with "two fairy godmothers, one grey-haired, the other blue-eyed."

Madame d'Abbadie's letters to Thérèse were filled with suggestions and advice to improve the prospective fiancée's appearance. "Please send me a photograph of yourself," she wrote. "I will choose one [to forward to Brazzà], or what is more likely, I will send them all back to you, displeased with your outfit and hairstyle…"

Thérèse must have found it challenging to put up with "Baddie," as she called her, but this brutally frank yet well-intentioned matron was her only link to the man of her dreams. The matchmaker continued writing to Brazzà, praising Thérèse's confident, willing nature and resolute character, which everyone attributed to her American education. Thérèse, a great-granddaughter of General Lafayette, had grown up in Washington, D. C., where her father had long been a legal counsel to the Embassy of France.

In March 1895 Brazzà was in Algeria. His health was improving, and he planned to return to France within a few weeks. He read Madame d'Abbadie's letters with interest. "Do you remember," she wrote, "a long conversation you had at Madame Cochin's house, with three older ladies and a young person? *That was she.* Do you remember the young lady sitting to your left at the Montalemberts' dinner? *That was she.*" Brazzà did not remember Thérèse, but he was beginning to wish he could.

The first days of April brought another near-catastrophe. On the road to Saïda, in northwestern Algeria, Brazzà's coach was in a terrible accident. "Coming back from Laghouat," he reminisced to Thérèse in a letter four years later, "where I had nearly had my back broken in the coach accident, [I found] a letter from Madame d'Abbadie along with the simple lines you had written, that expressed so clearly all your constancy and affectionate devotion ... at that moment, I decided to make you my wife."

A week later, filled with an anticipation he had never known, Brazzà sailed for France.

CHAPTER TWELVE -- THE BRIDEGROOM

Only a few years after the centennial celebration of the storming of the Bastille and the birth of the French Republic, currents of popular discontent were widespread in France. Throughout the 1890s, the French government was rocked by scandals and terrorist attacks.

Ferdinand de Lesseps' Panama Canal Company went bankrupt, generating a loss of one and a half billion francs and ruining many small investors. Army General and Minister of War Georges Boulanger, who had become immensely popular as "General Revenge," head of the nationalist opposition, made an attempt to topple the French government before fleeing to Belgium and committing suicide on the tomb of his mistress. In late 1894, by means of forged evidence, Captain Alfred Dreyfus was convicted of spying for Germany, expelled from the French army, and sentenced to forced labor at Devil's Island.

Politicians and ordinary citizens alike lived in fear of terrorist attacks. A French anarchist known as Ravachol, led to the guillotine in 1892 after several anti-government attacks, had come to symbolize the anarchist movement. In 1893, Auguste Vaillant hurled a bomb into the inner circle of the National Assembly, and the following year, French president Sadi Carnot was assassinated in Lyon by the 21-year-old Italian anarchist Caserio. It was a time of intense suspicion and uncertainty.

But General Commissioner Pierre Savorgnan de Brazzà, arriving in Paris in April 1895, had little interest in France's social and political troubles. His thoughts were consumed by his upcoming meeting with Thérèse de Chambrun. Madame d'Abbadie was organizing a dinner for April 15th, when she would introduce the two romantic correspondents.

Of all the participants, the one who seemed most anxious for the evening to be a success was the hostess, who entreated Thérèse to arrange her hair differently and "please put on a little powder!" But no artifices were needed. The meeting between 34-year-old Thérèse and 43-year-old Pierre was everything they had hoped it would be. France's "national explorer" seemed thoroughly taken by his charming, sincere, and affectionate companion. "And the white dress looked wonderful," wrote Madame d'Abbadie approvingly to Thérèse the next day.

As April in Paris turned to May, Brazzà and Thérèse met almost daily, when Brazzà's health permitted. He began to regret having taken lodgings on the wooded outskirts of the city, so far from the Chambrun family home in downtown Paris.

"[The doctor] won't let me out today," wrote Brazzà in one of his frequent notes to Thérèse. "He'll be back soon to see if I can go out tomorrow. I miss you, dear Thérèse, and I love you. If I had known, I wouldn't have come to stay here."

By May their conversations were full of wedding plans. Brazzà spoke frankly of the challenges and dangers of life in Africa. Thérèse responded that she would be happy to share them. Brazzà also confided his frustrations at the current political situation and the increasing pressure from unscrupulous traders. He was already looking forward to retirement, and wanted Thérèse to know that he might submit his resignation very soon. This would mean less money, but enough to live on in Algiers, a place he loved and where he would like to settle. She found it all very exciting. They both loved children, and looked forward to raising a family.

The wedding date was set for August 12, 1895. Since Thérèse had lost her grandmother earlier that year, a simple, intimate ceremony was planned. The bride's uncle Aldebert de Chambrun proposed that the wedding be held in the small gothic chapel he had recently had built in his Paris mansion, the Hôtel Bourbon-Condé. Aldebert and his wife had always doted on their niece Thérèse, and the entire family was already fond of Pierre. Writing to Brazzà in July, Aldebert addressed him as "my nephew and adopted son."

Marie-Thérèse Virginie Françoise Pineton de Chambrun and Pierre Paul François Camille Cergneu Savorgnan de Brazzà exchanged their vows at noon in the exquisite Bourbon-Condé chapel, a replica of Paris' 13th-century Sainte-Chapelle, complete with stained-glass windows. Thirty or forty relations and close friends looked on, including Charles de Chavannes, the best man, and Noël Ballay, now Governor of French Guinea. As the organist played Beethoven and Mendelssohn, the radiantly joyful bride and groom united their hopes, dreams, and lives.

After a festive meal the newlyweds departed for a honeymoon in Switzerland, then traveled to Italy where they were warmly received by Brazzà's large family. In September they sailed for Algeria, and during this short stay Thérèse came to know the southern Mediterranean coast that was so dear to her husband's heart. Twenty-four years earlier, as a midshipman, Brazzà had come ashore here on his first assignment to the exotic African continent. Thérèse shared his fascination for the Casbah, the old quarter of Algiers. They agreed to make their retirement home there.

Brazzà and Thérèse spent the last months of 1895 in Paris, making official visits and preparing for their move to French Congo *en famille*. Announcements of their wedding and future plans had appeared in scores of European newspapers, and Brazzà's social image had evolved from that of dashing explorer to contented husband in a glamorous couple. Already an Italian count, he had married into one of France's finest and richest noble families. American newspapers also gave the union prominent coverage, since Thérèse still had many devoted friends in the United States from her girlhood days in Washington.

In October, the French bicycle magazine *Le Vélo* reported that Brazzà had been won over by the new and highly popular form of transportation. " 'I left Paris in 1888, before the [1889] World's Fair,' " the article quoted him as saying. " 'No trace of bicycles then, or very few! After six or seven years in the Congo, I've returned to Paris, and everyone is riding bikes through the streets. I was amazed the first few days! Then I decided to try it too, what the devil! ...And I did.' " The reporter added that it took Monsieur de Brazzà less than twenty minutes to learn to ride.

The immense popularity of bicycles in Europe, however, was having dreadful consequences for Africa. The demand for rubber tires skyrocketed, and traders in the Congo Free State resorted to more and more brutal methods to obtain the raw material they needed in order to satisfy, and profit from, the expanding market. There were reports that many Africans were fleeing from Leopold's colony to French Congo, where they knew they would find refuge. Missionaries, European travelers like Mary Kingsley, and finally a few journalists began reporting on the stark contrast between Leopold's heinous abuses and Brazzà's humane methods. The King of the Belgians, already displeased by Brazzà's plans to build a French railway that would compete with his Leopoldville-to-Matadi line, was absolutely outraged at the comparison, which he saw as a public humiliation. He vowed to use every means in his power to put an end to Brazzà's career.

The first days of 1896 saw the General Commissioner and his new bride settling into married life in Libreville. Thérèse adapted well to the equatorial climate and to the African lifestyle that differed so completely from anything she had ever experienced. Things had changed for Brazzà as well. His professional responsibilities, though still tremendously important, were no longer the only focus of his life. He now had the loving support of a partner to help him through the difficult times -- and they would begin soon enough.

Brazzà had very few powerful contacts left in the French government, and little inclination to develop new ones. Louis de Montaignac, Jules Ferry, and Ferdinand de Lesseps had all died within the last several years. France's current president, Félix Faure, was a close friend of Leopold's. It was widely known that the Belgian monarch's financial interests controlled several French newspapers, particularly the influential *Figaro*. All Brazzà could do was manage his projects in the colony as best he could, until the time seemed right for his retirement. He was assisted by the capable Albert Dolisie, who had replaced Charles de Chavannes as lieutenant-governor of French Congo. Health problems had obliged Chavannes to retire to France in 1894.

In February 1896 Brazzà was informed by an official letter from the Minister of the Colonies that a military mission to link France's West African possessions with the Nile was imminent. The operation had been entrusted to Captain Jean-Baptiste Marchand, and the General Commissioner was requested to furnish transportation, hire porters, and facilitate the troops' passage through French Congo and Ubangi-Shari. The Marchand Mission closely resembled a proposal that Brazzà had made to the French government years earlier, seemingly without a very enthusiastic response, and he wondered what had stimulated the sudden approval of this new endeavor.

The apparently patriotic undertaking had in fact been strongly encouraged by the King of the Belgians. In order to divert attention from the brutality and exploitation in his personally-owned colony, and to prevent the other European powers from joining forces against him, Leopold had fanned the flames of France's eternal rivalry with Britain. The British already possessed the world's largest colonial empire, ran his argument. Why should they have free reign in Egypt, Sudan, and the entire Nile Valley? This challenge to France's pride, combined with Leopold's influence over the French president and over a number of strategically-placed journalists, managed to swing both governmental and popular opinion in favor of Marchand's Congo-to-Nile Mission.

The cost of the mission's transportation and other expenses would be enormous, and more than half the amount would eventually come out of Brazzà's meager budget. Planning the logistics of Marchand's 2000-mile trek across equatorial Africa with 200 men required a considerable investment of time as well. The General Commissioner spent many hours determining the most efficient and economic ways to transport the mission's personnel and huge cargo of supplies over some of the continent's most difficult terrain.

Arriving in Libreville in mid-July 1896, the imperious Captain Marchand was scandalized by Brazzà's patient diplomacy and unhurried, African-style business negotiations. Why was the General Commissioner bothering to haggle about prices and quantities with local merchants and traders? Why not simply requisition all the supplies and porters that the mission required? In his reports to Paris, Marchand roundly criticized Brazzà's "negrophile politics" and implied a serious lack of patriotism.

Like Stanley before him, 33-year-old Marchand had risen from humble beginnings, and was intent on making his mission a success by any means necessary. In August he informed Brazzà that he was ready to call a halt to his highly important military assignment and return to France unless he was granted complete civil authority over all the territories through which his convoy would pass, for the duration of his mission. Not without misgivings, Brazzà consented.

The result was disastrous. Over the next eighteen months, as the mission made its way through French Congo and Ubangi-Shari, inhabited by tribes loyal to Brazzà and to France, Marchand's men pillaged, burned, and executed at will under the pretext of procuring essential supplies and manpower as quickly as possible. Brazzà and Lieutenant-

Governor Dolisie were furious, but they could do nothing. Marchand had been granted temporary civil authority over these territories, and was carrying out a mission that the French government considered to be of primary strategic importance. The captain sent all his reports and requests for official support directly to the Minister of the Colonies in Paris, totally disregarding Brazzà's authority over the territories.

Ironically, the Marchand Mission ended in humiliation for France. After making his way across the African continent and occupying Fashoda throughout the blistering hot summer of 1898, the captain and his 200 men were confronted in September by the arrival of Kitchener's superior British force of 1500. Kitchener met with Marchand to seek a diplomatic resolution to the issue, and the ensuing standoff actually brought France and Britain to the brink of war. Finally, in December, Marchand and his men were ordered simply to evacuate their camp at Fashoda and return to France.

Examining the colonies' budget, Brazzà soon realized that Marchand's passage had brought him not only political and personal frustration, but financial ruin. The mission's colossal unanticipated expenditures had dealt a fatal blow to an already desperate fiscal situation. The General Commissioner had never been brilliant at managing money, but the unresponsive attitude and unreasonable demands of the bureaucrats in Paris had brought the colonies' finances to the crisis point. Year after year, when the promised "credits" from the Ministries were not forthcoming, Brazzà had continued to order necessary supplies and equipment, often covering the deficits with large amounts from the Savorgnan family fortune. Pierre's sister Marianna, with whom he corresponded frequently, had contributed most of her dowry to further her brother's plans for African development. But Brazzà's warnings about the colonies' precarious financial situation went unheeded in the Paris ministries. The French government continued to assign unrequested and largely unnecessary upper-grade administrators to serve -- and earn generous salaries -- in the colonies. Maintenance expenses for telegraph lines formerly paid by the Ministry of Telecommunications were transferred to Brazzà's colonial budget. The upkeep of the hospital ship *Minerva* and the coastal guard stations, until recently the responsibility of the Ministry of the Navy, now had to be settled by the General Commissioner.

By 1897, Brazzà was reporting a deficit of 2,250,000 francs on a budget of 3,700,000, an outrageous figure that his detractors in the government were only too glad to transmit to the press. Reading virulent articles alleging corruption and mismanagement in the Congo colony, French taxpayers were understandably incensed. Public opinion began to turn against the once-idolized "national explorer." According to some of France's best-known editorialists, Brazzà was nothing but a tyrant, a profiteer, and a negrophile, making use of his colony's isolation and conspiring with the Africans to waste and disperse France's generous subsidies.

And after all, wondered certain columnists, was General Commissioner Brazzà even a true Frenchman? Newspaper articles began emphasizing his Italian origins, his membership in the secret brotherhood of Freemasons, and his plans to retire in Algiers. Some journalists alleged that Brazzà had already converted to Islam. There were rumors that he planned to emigrate to Turkey or Greece, and seek political office there.

In March, Minister of the Colonies André Lebon ordered Brazzà to return to Paris immediately to justify his budget deficit and his financial and administrative management. Among the most serious of the many accusations facing the General Commissioner was one from the French Army, who maintained that the failure of the Congo-to-Nile Mission was entirely due to Brazzà's inability to have Marchand's supplies transported across central Africa quickly and efficiently.

Behind the various accusations, however, lurked several thinly-veiled ulterior motives. King Leopold's campaign to discredit Brazzà, have him replaced with a more tractable colonial governor, and thereby bring French Congo into line with the brutal, violent, and illegal practices rife in the Congo Free State, was succeeding. Greedy French traders rejoiced at the hope that they would soon be allowed to reap unlimited profits from slave labor in their country's own colony, unfettered by Brazzà's humanitarian imperatives. And the French Army, sinking deeper and deeper into the mire of international scandal generated by the irregularities of the Dreyfus trial, sought to use Brazzà as a scapegoat to avoid further criticism of the Marchand Mission.

In any case, Brazzà had little choice but to return to France, as his health was deteriorating. His liver problem was now complicated by malaria. Returning to Paris in April 1897, he divided the following months between doctors' appointments and meetings with government officials and newspaper editors. Brazzà was glad to speak to ministers and the press about the challenges he had faced, the decisions he had made, and the accomplishments of which he was justly proud. But he sensed that no one was listening, and that his eventual removal and disgrace were somehow inevitable.

France's erstwhile "national explorer" was amazed at the ferocity of the attacks against him, appearing in the same newspapers that had heaped praises on him in years past. Deeply offended, more for the honor of his family name than for himself, he maintained a cordial and dignified stance toward all.

Although many bureaucrats whispered rumors of Brazzà's impending dismissal, no one in the government dared to mention it directly to the General Commissioner himself. In the midst of a season of uncomfortable silence, the prestigious French Academy decided to make an unequivocal gesture. On November 18, 1897, in a solemn ceremony under the dome of their magnificent palace along the quais of the Seine, the Academy presented Brazzà with the Audiffred Prize in recognition of his "tireless ardor and consummate judgement, calm bravery and unequalled tenacity" in the exploration and administration of the colonies. It was "with great respect for the laws of humanity," stated the speaker, Auguste Himly, that Brazzà had created "a new African France."

Only a few steps from the modest *Petite Vache* restaurant, where Brazzà had found a warm welcome and encouragement for his first mission in 1875, his adopted country's most distinguished intellects had renewed their faith in him.

Brazzà and Thérèse ended the year in Algiers, where marital bliss and the gentle North African winter helped to ease his health problems and frayed nerves. He had had no official word from Paris about his dismissal, but the recent appointment of Lamothe, former Governor of Senegal, as "Interim General Commissioner" for French Congo made the government's intentions clear enough.

By January 1898 Brazzà's health had improved a bit. His professional life was still a matter of conjecture, and as he and Thérèse dined one evening with Monsieur Lépine, the Governor General of Algeria, they heard nothing further. The next day, the couple took their usual morning walk, and Brazzà bought his daily newspaper. As he opened it, he was stunned to see an article announcing his dismissal from his post in French Congo.

He and Thérèse were seated at a sidewalk café, and the Mediterranean wind became so strong that they were obliged to go inside the bar to read the story in full. If the printed report was true, then that was that. Brazzà's thirty years of naval service had come to an end, and this is how he had learned it -- in a bar in Algiers, on a windy day, from an anonymous newspaper article.

A few days later his official notification arrived, a dryly brief telegram from Minister of the Colonies André Lebon: "I have the honor of informing you that by a decision of 2 January 1898, I have discharged you from your functions as of 13 January, the date on which your current convalescence leave ends."

Brazzà's enemies could rejoice. The former General Commissioner was now no more than a French navy lieutenant without an assignment. But he was no longer the heavy-hearted midshipman of 1878 whose disappointment at his lost rank had sent him sailing down a flight of stairs. At age 46, Brazzà had a loving wife to share his joys and sorrows, and if one chapter of his life had reached its end, another was just beginning.

CHAPTER THIRTEEN -- THE FATHER

While Brazzà pondered his dismissal in private, the fate of another devoted French military officer was becoming highly public.

On January 13, 1898, the very same day Brazzà was discharged from his functions, the eminent novelist Emile Zola published an open letter to the French President on the front page of the liberal daily newspaper *l'Aurore*. Zola's letter, entitled "I Accuse," denounced the irregularities of the trial that had falsely convicted the Jewish officer Captain Alfred Dreyfus of espionage.

Dreyfus' military career and personal life were equally irreproachable. During the three years that the disgraced captain had spent in solitary confinement at Devil's Island, evidence in favor of his innocence had mounted. The identity of the real spy was known to several French officers, but in an effort to protect itself from yet another scandal, the army administration conspired to conceal the traitor. A military investigator attempting to vindicate Dreyfus had been silenced with a transfer to a remote post in southern Tunisia. Dreyfus' family and friends continued to press for a new trial, and now, in 1898, Zola's manifesto gave the matter renewed public attention.

Soon most of French society was divided into two camps, the liberal *Dreyfusards*, who supported human rights causes and mistrusted the military administration, and the conservative *Anti-Dreyfusards*, who proclaimed their nationalistic and anti-Semitic doctrines. The country's newspapers quickly took sides on the issue, and began publishing vehement diatribes for or against the imprisoned captain. The atmosphere of suspicion that had dominated France throughout the 1890s engendered virulent strains of xenophobia and anti-Semitism, and there were numerous attacks on Jewish businesses.

Finally, the suicide note of a French army colonel in September 1898 revealed that the original piece of evidence that had convicted Dreyfus was a forgery. After an additional eight years of retrials and appeals, the innocent captain was eventually acquitted, reinstated in the army, and promoted in 1906.

Dreyfus' case and Brazzà's are not without their similarities. Both marked a crisis point in the French government's murky campaign to disguise an increasing number of corruption and other scandals in the final years of the 19th century. Both affairs victimized patriotic military officers. Both Dreyfus and Brazzà were subjected to concerted slander campaigns in the right-wing French press, particularly in *le Figaro*, focusing on their ethnic and religious backgrounds. Dreyfus' Judaism, and Brazzà's birth in Italy and frequent convalescent stays in Algeria, were used as pretexts for accusations of disloyalty to France.

Ironically, it was Brazzà, the well-known public figure, who would be largely forgotten in the 20th century, while the modest Captain Dreyfus would come to symbolize the many victims of the era's injustice, prejudices, and institutionalized corruption.

Throughout 1898 Brazzà was content to settle into a peaceful oblivion in Algiers, far from the raging political conflicts in France. He and Thérèse had rented a house nestled in the hills overlooking the north African port. They named their new home *Dar-es-Sangha*, Arabic for "Home of the Sangha," after the central African river in one of the far reaches of the colony he had presented to France. Brazzà's health improved steadily. He gained weight and was no longer described as looking like "a skeleton." The past few difficult years were receding from their memories as the Count and Countess of Brazzà rejoiced at some happy news: they were expecting their first child.

Amid the pleasures of home and family, Brazzà still retained his enduring interest in equatorial Africa. He spent hours at his desk looking over his large maps, marking them with the most recent discoveries and colonial settlements. He suffered inwardly at the knowledge that immediately after his departure, his beloved French Congo had been divided into 42 concessions and quickly handed over to greedy rubber speculators to exploit as they saw fit. Brazzà made no public statement on the issue, but he kept informed of the situation through friends' letters and visits.

Albert Dolisie, an excellent colleague since 1883 and Brazzà's last Lieutenant-Governor of French Congo, began making arrangements to retire to France soon after the *grand commandant*'s dismissal. He arrived in his home town of Orléans directly from Africa in January 1899, but apparently the abrupt change of climate severely aggravated his chronic lung congestion. Much to his family's shock and dismay,

Dolisie passed away only five days after his arrival, at the age of 42.

Notified by telegram at the Chambrun's home in Paris, where Thérèse was just entering labor, Brazzà hurried to Orléans where he spent his 47th birthday delivering the eulogy at the funeral of one of his most dedicated comrades.

Brazzà returned to the welcome sight of his infant son, born during his six-hour absence. The new parents named the boy Jacques after Brazzà's sadly missed younger brother, the gifted naturalist.

A period of great happiness had begun for Pierre and Thérèse, who enjoyed every moment spent with their child. Life now began to follow a pleasant rhythm of winters in Algiers and summer visits with relatives in Italy and France. The couple's second son, Antoine, was born in 1900.

Every so often, when speaking to an acquaintance or reading an article, Brazzà would hear news of French Congo, and the news was increasingly alarming. Violent abuse, torture, and imprisonment of the tribesmen and their families had become commonplace. Some reports said that so many villages had been burned that the territory now resembled a vast wasteland. It had been barely three years since Brazzà's departure.

What had happened? Slowly but surely, the concessionary system practiced in King Leopold's Congo Free State had spread to France's African colonies. By 1899 the French government had legalized the attribution of huge parcels of land to private investors who were given complete sovereignty over their territories, and exclusive rights to all natural resources. One concession granted to a French investor in the Upper Ogoway region of Gabon was, incredibly, one-fifth the size of France.

For a period of 99 years, the investor was empowered to exploit his concession as he saw fit, and was fully authorized to establish his own laws and legal system, employ his own police force, levy taxes, etc., free from any control or inspection by French authorities. Africans were required to sell their produce and merchandise only to the investor's concessionary company, and on his terms, in flagrant violation of the principle of free trade on which the European powers had agreed at the Berlin Conference.

In theory, France required the concessionary companies to build and maintain local transportation, postal, and telegraph systems; to pay fees and a percentage of their earnings to the French government; and to allow a number of "native reservations" where the tribesmen could live, supposedly undisturbed. But no provision was made to enforce these rules. Brazzà, the "Father of Slaves," had conveniently been eliminated from the scene, and France's conscience had disappeared with him.

Europeans anxious for quick profits, and often already in debt, routinely arrived in Africa expecting to find a docile, submissive work force, and precious raw materials at every turn. They were amazed to discover tribal societies endowed with highly-developed cultures and centuries of history behind them. The tribesmen, accustomed to their own traditional methods of hunting, gathering, and agriculture, were not amenable to the thankless slave labor proposed by the concessionary companies.

And as for Africa's riches, they were not simply there for the taking. Ivory was precious and hard to come by, and valuable hardwoods were difficult to transport. Rubber trees needed to age seven years before producing the all-important latex fluid, which in turn had to be drained carefully so as not to harm the trees.

But the concessionary companies were not interested in learning the ways of French Congo's land and culture, and trying to work in harmony with them as Brazzà had done. After coming this far, they wanted immediate profits, and the only way to get them was through violent means. Often employing African mercenaries as foremen, they forced the tribesmen into a system of slave labor by beating, torturing, or murdering any who rebelled. Workers were often chained or yoked together, and whipping became common. Women and children were taken hostage and confined to camps to prevent the laborers from fleeing.

The humanitarian disaster was matched by an ecological catastrophe. Scorning the traditional method of draining the rubber trees and replanting for future harvests, the companies hacked and decimated the forests. Rebellious villages were routinely burned. Vast areas of fertile land were laid waste. The nightmare that Brazzà had long feared, and that he had worked so hard to prevent, was now a reality. But many people in the French establishment were still doing their utmost to keep that reality hidden from public view.

In 1901, former Minister of the Colonies André Lebon published a book entitled *La Politique de la France en Afrique* (*French Policy in Africa*) containing bitter attacks on Brazzà's colonial administration and a defense of the government's support of the concessionary system. Brazzà, who had been named "Honorary General Commissioner" by Lebon's successor Guillain, decided that the time had come to respond to the accusations, and state his opinions on the current situation in French Congo.

He composed a long, detailed letter to the Ministry of the Navy (since Brazzà was still, theoretically, a naval officer), addressing criticisms raised by Lebon, the press, and some members of the business community, and demonstrating that their allegations were false. He expressed his outrage at the human rights abuses that had apparently overwhelmed the colony since his dismissal. Brazzà demanded reparation for the slanderous claims against him, and submitted his official request for retirement from the French navy. His letter was dated May 6, 1901. He would not begin to receive his retirement pension for another two years.

Brazzà's unclouded personal life continued to be his main source of support at this time. The couple's third son, Charles, was born in July 1901 during a visit to Thérèse's family at their country home in Marvejols, Lozère, in south central France. Brazzà maintained strong ties to his adopted country, and he kept abreast of political currents in Paris through the Chambruns and the Paris Geographical Society, of which he was still an active member. Although there had been no official word from the French government, rumor had it that Brazzà's long, detailed, and forceful letter to the Ministry of the Navy had met with considerable attention and respect. When the erstwhile "national explorer" celebrated his 50th birthday on January 25, 1902, several newspapers commemorated the event with articles honoring his life and work.

By 1903 Brazzà's public image had been restored. At the urging of several prominent statesmen, the French government had granted him a retirement pension of 10,000 francs annually, as "national compensation." It was a rare honor that had last been accorded to Louis Pasteur in 1874.

Brazzà's improved health permitted him to consider a second career. The Chambruns noted that a Senate seat for Lozère was currently vacant, and suggested that the retired explorer and administrator would make an excellent legislator. He took some preliminary steps toward candidacy, and addressed the municipal council in October 1903, but soon concluded that life in the political arena was not for him.

Thérèse had given birth to a daughter, Marthe, when tragedy struck the family. Four-year-old Jacques, the couple's eldest son, became ill with what was diagnosed as a digestive ailment. It was in fact acute appendicitis, and two days later the boy was dead. Pierre and Thérèse were inconsolable at the loss. All the pain and humiliation they had suffered in years past seemed like trifles compared to this.

"Poor little Jacques!" Brazzà wrote in a letter to Chavannes in early January 1904. "He came to fill our lives at the time we were most in need... Now he leaves us with a feeling of gratitude for the joy he brought us, and of regret that he had so little time to enjoy his own life...."

In their grief, Brazzà and Thérèse centered themselves on family life. Surrounded by pines and eucalyptus trees, *Dar-es-Sangha*, their home in Algiers, became more than ever a haven of peace and serenity. By now the house was filled with mementos and family gifts from France, Italy, and Africa. Brazzà had turned the basement into a little museum of his years spent in the bush -- his hammock, camp stool, rifle, the sextant that had so impressed the tribesmen in the early days, African carvings and artifacts, and the presents that Makoko and other rulers had given him -- all were kept as precious reminders of a place that had become an inextricable part of him.

So many people in his life had passed away... Noël Ballay, who had planned to buy a retirement home in Algiers near his old friend; the naturalist Alfred Marche, who had spent his last years as a government administrator in Tunis; and Brazzà's dear sister Marianna, who had written faithfully from Italy to her adventurous brother for all those years, and who had dreamed of coming to join him. Many colonial officers in French Congo had lost their lives to tropical illness, and the troubled Louis Mizon had committed suicide in 1899. Even the explorer's former rival, Henry Morton Stanley, was gone. After all his remarkable exploits in Africa, *Bula Matari* had died in England, of pneumonia.

While Brazzà retained his links with the past, the widely-celebrated new 20th century had brought no sweeping changes to the troubled state of French politics. Mistrust of religious and ideological differences still dominated society in general, and the administration in particular. The *Affaire Dreyfus* was years from a satisfactory conclusion, and had been joined by other scandals like the *Affaire des Fiches*. In this most recent revelation, it was learned that the military establishment, with the help of the Freemasons, had compiled secret files (or *fiches*) on the religious practices and political opinions of every French officer, and that these files had been used to determine promotions. Many French citizens were outraged, including Brazzà, who resigned from the Freemasons in protest. For years he had been a member of the conservative fraternity in name only.

News from French Congo was increasingly disturbing. The invention of the automobile had further increased the demand for rubber, and its production was draining the life blood of the African continent. The murder, torture, and mutilation of the Congo tribesmen had reached such a point that the local missionaries, in desperation, sent messengers to Brazzà's home in Algiers to beg him to take action.

Brazzà was horrified at the missionaries' reports, and their frightful stories haunted his thoughts. There was no question about it. The carnage had to be stopped. Something had to be done. But what? Brazzà had devoted years of his life to trying to halt the violent, frenzied greed of people like King Leopold II, and he had failed. Now, at his age, and with his diminished health, what could he do? The answer eluded him. But he certainly could not stand by and do nothing.

Brazzà was not alone. Humanitarian organizations like the British *Aborigines Protection Society* and the *Congo Reform Association* drew public attention to the abuses of the concessionary system in Africa. The popular British author Arthur Conan Doyle published *Crime in the Congo* about excesses in Leopold's personal colony. French human rights associations and liberal newspapers like *l'Humanité* published shocking stories of torture and exploitation.

Apologists for the concessionary companies countered by insisting that by means of the rubber trade, Europeans were replacing Africa's native vices of cannibalism, ignorance, and idleness with the civilized virtues of Christianity, security, and industry. Forced labor, and the high "native tax" that the tribesmen were obliged to pay in rubber or other local products on pain of death or mutilation, were a reasonable price to pay for the "services rendered" by the European occupation of Africa, claimed conservative journalists.

By 1904, the horrible charade was deceiving virtually no one. More and more first-hand reports appeared in the press, revealing more and more gruesome tales of abuse.

Two of the most appalling incidents occurred in Ubangi-Shari, the present-day Central African Republic.

In Bangui, 68 women and children hostages were crowded into a hut with no ventilation as a means of forcing their husbands and fathers to work. When they were freed weeks later, 45 had died of asphyxiation. Weakened, malnourished, and mortally ill, 19 more passed away within days. Only one woman and one child survived the ordeal.

Meanwhile, in Fort Crampel, two French civil servants named Toqué and Gaud presided over a macabre celebration of France's national day on July 14, 1903. Instead of lighting fireworks, Gaud inserted a stick of dynamite into the anus of a tribesman named Papka, and blew him to bits in front of his family. Far from regretting his action, the sadistic Gaud claimed that such practices "kept the Blacks from making trouble."

When reports of these atrocities appeared in European newspapers, the long-misled French public was revolted and horrified. Their outcry demanded an end to this public shame. The Ministry of the Colonies was forced to admit that it had made an abominable error in condoning the concessionary companies' ignoble practices for so long. In trying to avoid the most recent and most heinous in a long series of political and military scandals, the French government had reached its lowest point in the moral spectrum, not only in the view of its own citizens, but in the eyes of the entire world.

Clearly, some sort of high-profile action would have to be taken in order to cleanse the Republic's tarnished image. The administration would order an inspection of French Congo, led by someone that the public considered trustworthy and equitable. Of course, the inspector would have to have a background in colonial affairs; he would have to "know the ropes," and understand the way government business was carried out. The bureaucrats sought someone who had come out of their system, but who could present a reassuring face to the French public, and to the world. Who was capable of this critical mission?

French President Émile Loubet suggested Brazzà. The former General Commissioner was a well-known advocate of African rights, popular with the French people, and more familiar than anyone with the French Congo, the colony he himself had created. Above all, he was outside politics. Minister of the Colonies Étienne Clémentel was mistrustful of the president's choice. In the wake of the political fallout from the Toqué-Gaud Scandal, the last thing his office needed was to have more dreadful crimes dug up by a negrophile like Brazzà.

But the fact remained that Brazzà projected the popular image the mission required, and his age and health problems would probably prevent him from seeing more than the colonial administrators wanted him to see. After all, this would be a tightly-controlled inspection, not the kind of searing exposé that the British Consul Roger Casement had written about King Leopold II's Congo Free State a year or two earlier, and that the British had been foolish enough to publish. The French government would keep a close eye on Brazzà.

President Loubet and Minister Clémentel wrote to the former explorer, requesting that he lead the government's mission of inspection in French Congo. Brazzà's response was immediate and positive. As the "Father of Slaves," how could he decide otherwise?

Thérèse, her family, and many friends and acquaintances spent days trying to change Brazzà's mind. Had he forgotten the ill-treatment and ingratitude he and his colleagues had received at the hands of the French government? Did he not realize that the faithful sergeant Malamine had effectively died of starvation and lack of medical care in Senegal, while his retirement pension was held up in Paris? And what of Brazzà's health -- his liver and bronchial problems? After decades of tropical dysentery, malaria, and exhaustion, the explorer's white hair and stooped posture made him appear much older than his 52 years.

Besides the difficulties of the journey itself, what sort of reception would Brazzà's findings of corruption and human rights abuses in the colonies receive when he returned to France? Would the conservative press launch another campaign of vicious personal attacks? Would Brazzà and his family receive threats from pro-government and pro-business partisans? After all, only a few years earlier the novelist Émile Zola, who had courageously denounced the irregularities of the Dreyfus trial, had died under mysterious circumstances shortly after his return from exile in England.

In the face of all these arguments, Brazzà's conviction was unshakeable. He would return to the Congo to try to right the terrible wrongs that France had committed there. He had created the colony with great hopes and plans for its future, and now all of his and the chieftains' promising projects had been nullified by merciless greed. As Brazzà saw it, it was his inescapable duty to Congo, and to France, to make some sense of the situation, and to ensure that something was done before the African peoples and cultures he had known and loved were destroyed forever.

Thérèse set one condition on her husband's departure: that she would go with him. The dire premonitions that haunted her thoughts would not allow her to let her husband undertake the fateful trip alone. Wrenching as it was to be apart from the three young children left to them, Thérèse and Pierre decided that Antoine, Charles, and Marthe would spend the six months allotted for the mission with their affectionate grandmother in Rome.

The die was cast. Brazzà, the "Father of Slaves," would go to meet his destiny in Africa, with Thérèse by his side.

CHAPTER FOURTEEN -- THE INVESTIGATOR

Visitors to Paris in 1905 admired a capital flourishing with early 20th-century innovations. Gustave Eiffel's distinctive tower, built as a temporary attraction for the 1889 World's Fair and originally ridiculed as the "metal asparagus," had become so popular that it was now a permanent part of the city's landscape. Traditional horse-drawn carriages and buses were rivaled by bicycles, a few automobiles, and the capital's five-year-old *Métropolitain*, the underground rail network.

Parisians gathered in theaters to watch images of world events on cinematic newsreels, and France's first movie studio was being built at Buttes Chaumont in northeast Paris. Police stations were equipped with telephones, and much to the dismay of French burglars and ruffians, detectives were now able to identify criminals by their fingerprints.

The new century would bring sweeping moral changes as well. The evolution of one Frenchman's attitude toward colonialism is eloquently described in a personal reminiscence published in 1935 by the writer and philosopher Félicien Challaye, a member of Brazzà's 1905 investigative mission to Congo.

7. Brazzà in early 1905, the last year of his life. Photograph courtesy of the Bibliothèque Nationale de France, Paris.

"Thirty-five years ago," wrote Challaye in *Souvenirs sur la colonisation* (*Memories of Colonization*), "when I went on the first of my long journeys, I naïvely believed what I had been taught in France's schools. I believed that colonialism was a humanitarian enterprise, destined to advance peoples of inferior races through contact with white civilization. I believed that these backward peoples sought the help of whites, and that they were grateful for this well-intentioned aid. I believed that France was the most benevolent of all the colonial powers, and that the loyalty of her subjects bore witness to their gratitude.

"A few experiences in the course of my first trip around the world gave rise to my first doubts on the human value of the colonial régime. These doubts gathered more and more strength the more closely I studied the situation of various colonies. Finally I was confronted by a certainty exactly the opposite of my first hypothesis: colonization is not a humanitarian enterprise. It is a régime of political oppression aimed at the economic exploitation of a subjugated people."

Decades would pass, however, before this realization gained the least currency in French society. In 1905, the European colonization of Africa was still accepted as a viable and respectable idea. Pierre Savorgnan de Brazzà had been enlisted to investigate the abuses of French colonialism in Congo, not to incriminate the system itself.

But as he made his way to the Ministry of the Colonies' elegant headquarters in the Pavillon de Flore wing of the Louvre, Brazzà was beginning to wonder exactly what he was expected to investigate. Minister Clémentel and many of his subordinates were openly hostile to the newly-reinstated General Commissioner. Brazzà's requests for the files and information he needed to prepare the inquiry, such as the complaints and testimonies of the Congo tribesmen, often met with delays or outright denials. The situation became so antagonistic that after his first few visits, Brazzà never entered the Ministry of the Colonies without a companion who could serve as a witness. Every evening Brazzà and his assistant each wrote out a personal record of what had transpired that day, and compared their notes.

Purely by chance, Brazzà learned that another investigative mission, staffed by government insiders, was to be sent to French Congo at the same time as his own. If the other mission's findings disagreed with Brazzà's, the two sets of data would cancel each other out, or so the Ministry of the Colonies hoped.

As soon as he heard of the scheme, Brazzà stipulated that there would be only one mission, or else he would refuse to participate. After considerable discussion, the duplicate mission was cancelled. At least, reasoned the bureaucrats, the Ministry could still profit from Brazzà's image as a patriotic hero and a champion of Africans' rights. Maybe his trip to the colonies would divert the French public's attention from the current mess of troublesome domestic and European issues.

But as the mission's departure date approached, Brazzà's relations with the Ministry of the Colonies became even more strained. "I have the distinct impression," he confided to his family, "that the Minister regrets having chosen me for this investigation." The General Commissioner was informed that many of the files he had asked to see either did not exist, or were "unavailable." He was notified that the duration of his mission must not exceed six months. Subtracting a month's travel time in each direction, that left only four months to cover a wide area of the colony, a challenging proposition even for a young and healthy person, let alone someone of the retired explorer's age and health.

Fortunately, Brazzà was able to assemble an excellent staff of fourteen men that included Inspector General of the Colonies Hoarau-Desruisseaux, the gifted writer and educator Félicien Challaye, several highly dependable administrators, and a military doctor.

As with Brazzà's African expeditions in years past, the preparations for his investigative mission were duly reported in the press, and he was once again a highly popular figure in France. He received letters of encouragement from average French citizens, as well as some words of warning from those who knew of the corruption and violence in the colonies. One letter advised Brazzà that a certain family of French concessionaires in Congo were "fearsome assassins and thieves ... [with their questionable earnings] they are having a vast mansion built for themselves [in France]. Be sure to take great care for your personal safety."

Brazzà's close friends, including Charles de Chavannes, made a final concerted effort to discourage him from undertaking the dangerous mission, but Brazzà was adamant. Thérèse, proud of her husband's integrity but troubled by dire premonitions, was still determined to accompany him. The devoted parents confided five-year-old Antoine, three-year-old Charles, and two-year-old Marthe to their governess Adèle, who would care for the three children during their six-month stay with Pierre's mother in Rome.

The mission sailed from Marseilles on April 5, 1905. Several official letters, however, outdistanced the investigators. Quite obviously, Minister of the Colonies Clémentel had never supported Brazzà's inquiry, and had allowed the mission to proceed only at the urging of President Loubet. Several Ministry bureaucrats had written to Congo Commissioner Émile Gentil, Brazzà's successor, to reassure him that neither he nor the concessionary system had anything to fear.

As far as the French government was concerned, the concessions were the only way to compel Congo, often viewed as the "Cinderella" of France's African colonies because of its extreme poverty and insalubrious climate, to turn a profit. Gentil was instructed to welcome Brazzà and his team with every courtesy, but to make sure they followed a carefully pre-determined itinerary. "We are depending on your administration," wrote the Paris bureau chief for concessions to Gentil in late March, "to provide an outlet for [Brazzà's] ardor, which his age seems to have increased without clearing his head."

On April 29th, Brazzà stepped ashore at Libreville to an ardent welcome by the Gabonese people. It had been thirty years since his arrival here, in the "City of the Free," as an enthusiastic young ensign at the head of his first African expedition. Now he was grey-haired and stooped with age, but his eyes still shone as he recognized old friends. Former slaves that he had liberated decades earlier knelt at his feet with their families. Onlookers sang and cheered. *Rocamambo*, the *grand commandant*, had returned!

A few days later, as tom-toms carried news of their arrival along the coast and through the forest, Brazzà and his party boarded a steamer that carried them up the Ogoway River. In the villages where they stopped, chieftains came to greet the "Father of Slaves" and tell him of the dismal changes that had overtaken the colony since his departure. Félicien Challaye was struck by the instant rapport between the tribesmen and Brazzà, whose manner was a mixture of friendliness, respect, and close attention to detail. The General Commissioner took the time to listen carefully to each testimony and complaint.

The chieftains all asked Brazzà for relief from the high "taxes" (*impôts*) -- which they referred to as "fines" (*amendes*) -- demanded by the concession companies. French law stated that the territories granted in concession belonged not to their African residents, but to the companies, who were perfectly entitled to require exorbitant "taxes" from the tribesmen. The amount was generally paid in balls of raw rubber. Additional rubber and other products that the tribesmen wished to sell were grossly undervalued by the companies, and were exchanged for overvalued, unfamiliar and usually undesirable European manufactured goods. Tribesmen who refused to cooperate with the system were whipped or shot. Rebellious villages were routinely burned. Many clans had retreated further and further into the forest to evade the companies. Brazzà noted that the Ogoway Valley seemed deserted compared to what it had been in years past.

When Brazzà tried to investigate certain complaints, he came up against a wall of official interference. Roads were blocked. Boats were delayed. As in Paris, the documents he requested had mysteriously disappeared. In some places, telegraph lines had been cut.

But every now and then a crack appeared in the colonial administration's defense, letting a little of the truth shine through. In the Ogoway village of Sindara, the local French authorities had neglected the official order to remove all chains from captive laborers for the duration of Brazzà's visit. The prisoners who came to unload the party's baggage were shackled. "The prisoners arrived chained two by two," noted Challaye in his journal. "The chain fixed around the neck of the first man went down his back, then across the chest of the second and around his neck."

The investigators continued on to Lambarene and Lope, through an increasingly bleak and deserted landscape. Brazzà thought back to the day in 1876 when he had purchased the freedom of a runaway slave, and had announced proudly that the French flag symbolized freedom. What did the tricolor symbolize now? he wondered bitterly. African tribes fled at the sight of a French camp, in order to escape the torture and murder committed with the tacit approval of Brazzà's adopted homeland.

Brazzà confided the rest of the investigation of Gabon to his second-in-command, Hoarau-Desruisseaux, and sailed with most of the party to the Congo Free State's port of Matadi. There they took the Belgian train to Leopoldville, located just across the Pool from Brazzaville, their destination. Since the completion of King Leopold's railroad at a cost of thousands of human lives, the arduous 240-mile journey from the coast to the Pool took only one day.

Arriving in Leopoldville on May 15th, already frustrated and saddened by what the past few weeks had shown him, Brazzà was further disheartened to be greeted only by a French missionary and a pair of low-level French officers. In his naïveté, what had he expected? That his successor, Congo Commissioner Emile Gentil, would rejoice at the investigator's arrival, and would travel across the Pool to welcome him?

Brazzà, Thérèse, and the rest of the party took the ferry across the Congo River to the city named for the *grand commandant*. Some Bateke tribesmen had turned out to meet him, but Brazzà was prevented from talking to them by the French administrators, who hurried him along.

Congo Commissioner Gentil had been instructed to receive the investigators courteously, and a banquet was held the next day. Though given in the visitors' honor, the event was dominated by the same chilling atmosphere of resentment that had haunted every aspect of the mission. Pale and sullen, Gentil refused to wear his dress uniform to the banquet as an act of disrespect to Brazzà.

While proposing a toast to his guest's health, Gentil made reference to his predecessor's "rather sudden departure" seven years earlier, and suggested that the explorer's return was a kind of "revenge." He went so far as to say that Brazzà should never have taken on the burden of investigating his former colleagues, "for he should learn from experience that one often has thankless tasks to perform, tasks for which one receives more criticism than praise."

The toast met with complete silence. French missionary Prosper Augouard, whose years of collaboration with Gentil and the concessionary system had graced him with the impressive title of Bishop of Brazzaville and Apostolic Vicar of Upper Congo, rose to give his address. He spoke respectfully of Brazzà's explorations, and then heaped praises on Gentil for crowning Brazzà's efforts with a long-awaited "economic impulse."

Outraged and insulted as Brazzà may have felt, at first he said nothing. Decades earlier he had easily shamed Stanley during the banquet at Paris' Continental Hotel. But now he was too depressed and ill to get into a brawl. Without even rising to his feet, Brazzà remarked that for his part he had "gone barefoot" while Augouard had lived and traveled comfortably under Stanley's protection. Incensed, the bishop called Brazzà's accusation a "calumny."

The next day's visit to a Catholic mission school in Brazzaville went more smoothly. The children lined up to sing a French chorus composed in honor of the great explorer, to the tune of the Italian song *Santa Lucia*:

> *Founder of cities,*
> *Peaceful conqueror,*
> *Franceville was founded*
> *By him in triumph.*
> *Brazzaville was born*
> *His beloved eldest daughter*
> *Monsieur de Brazzà,*
> *Monsieur de Brazzà.*

Pierre and Thérèse were deeply touched. If they were to have only one happy memory of the investigative mission, it would be this moment with the Congolese children at the mission school, by a grove of handsome mango trees, on a hill overlooking Brazzaville.

But the joyful moment was short-lived. Bishop Augouard, still piqued at Brazzà's "calumny" at the banquet, was even more offended when the free-thinking explorer did not include a word about God in his short address to the children. The missionary provoked Brazzà into a quarrel, and two men were soon arguing about their respective hardships and accomplishments of years past. The role of diplomat fell ultimately to Thérèse, who later managed to placate the bishop by attending morning Mass several times during the visit.

In late May the mission boarded the steamer *Albert Dolisie* on their way north to the Ubangi-Shari region, where the worst atrocities were said to have taken place. They sailed across the wide expanse of the Pool, passed the cliffs that Stanley had called "the White Cliffs of Dover," and entered the strait known as "the Corridor," where the Congo's tea-colored waters narrowed to only a mile or two.

Farther along the slow-moving, majestic river, the travelers saw it widen again to about a dozen miles. The Congo was marked by islands, floating water plants, and an occasional hippo or crocodile. Apart from a few riverside villages, its banks were covered by somber, silent tropical forests that varied from green to nearly black in the sweltering haze. Brazzà recognized the spot where twenty-five years earlier, after an exhausting march, he had seen the great river for the first time. He seemed to take heart as he described his first dramatic view of the moonlit Congo to his companions as "sublime ... a dream fulfilled."

They stopped for the night at Bolobo, a settlement on the Belgian left bank. The Protestant mission there was directed by the well-known British churchman and explorer George Grenfell, who had discovered the mouth of the Ubangi River in 1886. He came on board the *Dolisie* to greet Brazzà and was invited to stay for dinner. Asked how the tribesmen were being treated at Bolobo, Grenfell affirmed, "They aren't treated badly here. There's no rubber."

Grenfell warned them that once they entered the Ubangi River valley, in the heart of the rubber zone, they would find it deserted. The concession companies had no money to pay the thousands of workers they required, and they routinely resorted to kidnapping local women and children to force the tribesmen into slave labor. Several bloody rebellions had erupted, during the course of which the tribesmen had raided armories and procured weapons and powder, before retreating to their hiding places in the forest. All white men, as well as the brutal Senegalese Regional Guards who terrorized the Ubangi tribes, were considered targets. Brazzà and his mission would enter the Ubangi-Shari region at their own risk.

For Brazzà there was no question: the mission would pursue its original itinerary. His companions agreed. The *Dolisie* steamed into the milky-brown waters of the Ubangi and traveled up the tranquil river valley where, just as Grenfell had said, villages were few and far between. Even the animals and tropical birds seemed to keep silent.

The investigators approached the reportedly dangerous area of Bétou, where they disembarked and prepared to enter the village unarmed. As they walked, Thérèse noticed a small black child by the side of the trail, gathered the toddler up in her arms, and continued walking beside her husband. She was the first white woman ever to venture into Ubangi-Shari.

The mission was welcomed with tom-toms and singing. During a visit of several hours, Brazzà met with the chief while the other members of the party bought bracelets, necklaces, tribal fetishes, and other souvenirs, paying for them with small bags of salt.

The investigators continued on to Bangui, the regional capital. They were shown the hut where 68 women and children had been sequestered, and where most had died. The French administrator responsible for the tragedy had never been punished -- in fact, he had been transferred to Brazzaville, a much more desirable assignment.

After boarding smaller, more maneuverable boats to take them as far as Fort-de-Possel, the travelers undertook ten days on horseback to reach Fort-Crampel. For Brazzà, already suffering from dysentery, this was the most punishing leg of the journey. Nights were often spent in damp huts, and food was difficult to obtain. The mission endured pilferage and invasions of army ants. They waited out heavy rains and winds, and during a violent lightning storm, three members of the party received severe shocks.

But what weakened Brazzà most was an overwhelming sense of despair. The fertile plains that he had known as a young explorer were now a barren wilderness. Brazzà had convinced Makoko and the other chieftains to accept the French administration of equatorial Africa, and thirty years later, desolation and exploitation seemed to be the only result. Félicien Challaye wrote of his leader's torment:

"An immense sadness added to the weight of all this physical and intellectual exhaustion. Monsieur de Brazzà had a passionate love for this Congo which he had explored and given to France, then governed and organized. He suffered misery to find it in such a fearful state. He saw a tyrannical and greedy administration establish an ill-conceived and damaging system of taxes, and enforce it by proceedings that were often brutal, terrifying the natives, and driving them from the government posts instead of drawing the people to them by the offer of effective protection. He saw the concessionary companies, rapacious and cynical, trying to create a new form of slavery...."

As the mission approached the French post at Dékoa, Brazzà noticed some human remains left by the side of the road. He instructed the party to halt until the remains were given a decent burial. Prayers were said. They resumed the journey, but a question remained. Had the discovery of the bones been purely accidental? Was it some sort of warning, or perhaps a cry for help? That evening in Dékoa, the French official who hosted them tried to maintain a cheerful attitude, but he could barely hide his nervousness and apprehension at the investigators' presence.

After the evening meal, a tribal dance was presented to entertain the visitors. Seated on the ground in front of his hut, Brazzà had nearly given way to exhaustion when he noticed something unusual about the performance. While the tom-toms beat an implacable rhythm, the dancers formed a circle. One tribesman, his arms across his chest, fell to the ground and, squirming as if his feet were tied, began crawling on his belly like a captive attempting to escape. His expression and his movements grew more and more desperate as he crawled closer and closer to where Brazzà was sitting.

The white-haired explorer's face betrayed his emotion as he fit the pieces together -- the bones left by the side of the road -- the nervous official -- the dance of imprisonment and escape. Where were the slaves or hostages that his host was trying to conceal from him?

Interrupting the performance, Brazzà demanded the truth from the French administrator, who finally admitted that a new hostage camp had recently been established nearby. The investigators were taken to the site, not far from the regional post of Fort-Crampel. They discovered a concentration camp where the wives and children of forced laborers, including those who had danced for the guests, were crowded into huts in a camouflaged site patrolled by armed Regional Guards. At the arrival of the mission, all the hostages were freed -- for the time being.

Brazzà had seen enough. It was time to return to the French Congo's capital while he still had the energy to file a report of this most recent horror. Another ten-day trek on horseback brought the investigators to the Ubangi River, where they boarded the steamer back to Brazzaville. Nursed by Thérèse, Brazzà rested as much as possible and seemed to feel better, but soon after the party reached the capital, his dysentery worsened. He spent most of his last week in Brazzaville in his hut, moving from bed to an easy chair, where he wrote out messages to be telegraphed back to Paris, and tried to interview as many witnesses as possible before his departure.

During this last week of August 1905, the case of the two officials who had blown up a tribesman with dynamite in July 1903 had finally come to trial in Brazzaville. In place of the General Commissioner, who was too ill to leave his quarters, Challaye attended the proceedings, took careful notes, and reported the day's events to Brazzà every evening.

The trial of Toqué and Gaud attracted the attention of the entire French community in Brazzaville, most of whom considered the two men political scapegoats for an unfortunate but necessary state of affairs in colonial Africa. Georges Toqué, aged 26, a small, thin Breton with a nervous tic, was an ambitious colonial administrator, rather well-liked by both whites and blacks. Fernand Gaud, aged 31, was husky and dark-bearded, with a "bestial face," according to Félicien Challaye. Gaud had trained for several professions in his native Provence without much success, and had ended up as Toqué's clerk for native affairs at Fort-Crampel, where the tribesmen referred to him as "the savage beast."

Even after all he had seen and heard during the four-month investigation in the bush, Challaye was horrified by the nature and number of accusations against the two men. He was further appalled by the prevailing French attitude of contempt for the lives of Africans, whose murders were, he learned, classified as *animalicides*. The hostage-taking of native women, who were routinely raped by the Senegalese Regional Guards and infected with venereal diseases before falling prey to smallpox, starvation, or asphyxiation, had become common practice throughout the colony. Whipping was permitted by French colonial law. It was not until the foremen gave more than 25 lashes, or failed to stop when the blood ran, that the act could be called a crime, but such transgressions were rarely reported.

Toqué and Gaud were accused of a long list of tortures, killings, and brutalities. They did not even bother to deny many of the charges, which they maintained were fair punishments for tribesmen that they judged to be murderers, deserters, or traitors. Gaud freely admitted having placed prisoners in the "silo" (a deep, bottle-shaped hole in the ground whose narrow opening was covered with a canoe), but he denied depriving them of food or urinating on them. Toqué was accused of the murder of a chief named Ndagara, whom he had ordered to be thrown over a waterfall and drowned.

Toqué claimed that in the beginning he had written letters of complaint to France about the harsh way the natives were treated, but that he had been intimidated by his superiors to cover up the brutality by falsifying death records and other documents. "It was a general massacre, just to keep business going," he declared to the court.

The brutal dynamite killing of Papka was discussed in great detail. Toqué stated that Papka, employed as a guide, had led a French expedition into an ambush, causing the death of several men. Toqué had instructed Gaud to have Papka arrested and shot for treason. Instead, Gaud placed Papka in the "silo" for a few days.

On July 14, Gaud asked Toqué how they should celebrate the French national holiday. Sick in bed with a liver ailment, Toqué placed Gaud in temporary command of the post. He instructed Gaud to liberate two other captives, and to "do as he liked" with Papka. Toqué testified that he had intended these words to mean "Free him or keep him prisoner." Gaud, unfortunately, took the command literally. But Gaud claimed that the fatal stick of dynamite had been attached to the prisoner's neck, not inserted in his anus.

The prosecutor stated that, judging by the attitude of the two alleged murderers, they seemed to have no awareness whatsoever of the seriousness of their crimes. The defense attorney, a colonial administrator in Brazzaville, stressed the "terrible situation" in which the two men had been required to serve, in a remote and isolated central African post. Toqué and Gaud's principal white accuser, the French doctor Le Maout, had died of a liver ailment only three days before the trial began. Their principal black accuser, a Regional Guard named Yambissi, had himself been convicted of murder and sentenced to forced labor. Interestingly, he was the first Regional Guard ever to be punished for a crime.

The only other witness whose testimony carried any weight was Toqué's subordinate, a junior official named Chamarande. Revolted at the violence he had witnessed, the young Frenchman refused to be a part of the conspiracy of silence that had proved so effective for so long.

The verdict was announced at the end of the week. Most of the charges were dismissed, but the two men were each found guilty of one unpremeditated murder with extenuating circumstances: Toqué for the drowning of Ndagara, and Gaud for the dynamite killing of Papka. They were sentenced to five years in prison. As matters turned out, they would actually serve only two years of their sentences, and both would go on to publish successful books about their experiences.

The French community's reaction to the verdict was immediate. "This conviction provoked shock and indignation in Brazzaville," noted Challaye. "Most Frenchmen were amazed and furious that the lives of a few 'dirty niggers' could be estimated at such a price. In the crowd leaving the courtroom after the verdict, I heard a young civil servant shout, 'It's enough to make you turn nigger.'"

The investigative mission was nearing the end of its stay in Africa. Brazzà had concluded that the entire concessionary system in French Congo must be dismantled, and he had already sent numerous detailed telegrams to that effect back to Paris. His health was very weak, but his only concern now was returning to France to be able to file his report, complete with evidence and many testimonies, to the French government. Félicien Challaye, for his part, had sent regular reports to the major French daily newspaper *le Temps*.

Congo Commissioner Emile Gentil had been in a state of sullen nervous tension since the mission's arrival the previous April. Convinced that he would be held to account for seven years of monstrous human rights abuses in his colony, he left for France on August 27th in a desperate attempt to justify himself to the Ministry of the Colonies before it was too late.

As Pierre and Thérèse prepared to leave Brazzaville, they read the dispatches and personal mail that had arrived for them. A few weeks earlier, the Savorgnan di Brazzà family doctor in Rome had sent the parents a warm, cordial letter, written in Italian, with news of their three children.

"They are three little loves," wrote Dr. Tullio Rossi-Doria. "Marthe is exquisite and refined, and very charming. Antoine is sweet and affectionate, while Charles is a bit more reserved." Sadly, the three young children would never see their father again.

On August 29th, a litter was brought to carry Brazzà to the ferry on the far edge of town, but he insisted on walking. Leaning on Thérèse's arm, with a faltering step, and his face lost in a melancholy reverie, the white-haired explorer slowly made his way through the African city that bore his name.

The investigators boarded the ferry to Leopoldville and under a murky sky, Brazzà contemplated the wide waters of the Pool for the last time. The Belgian railroad brought the mission to Matadi, where the ship *Ville de Macéio* would take them back to Europe.

By the time they docked at Libreville, it was obvious to everyone that Brazzà was gravely ill. Dr. Cureau, the mission's physician, insisted that the patient be taken to the French military hospital at Dakar, if not to another clinic even sooner.

Sensing that his end was near, Brazzà formally placed Hoarau-Desruisseaux in charge of the investigative mission. Despite his weakened condition, he dictated an individual letter of commendation for every one of the 14 men who had accompanied him on the arduous and dangerous journey, recommending them for promotion or induction into the French Legion of Honor.

The *Ville de Macéio* continued its voyage up the West African coast, past Porto Novo, Abidjan, and Conakry, as Brazzà wavered on the edge of delirium. He entreated Hoarau-Desruisseaux to save "his" Congo from the shameful suffering they had all witnessed.

When the ship finally reached Dakar, Brazzà was set on a stretcher, his eyes vague, his cheeks hollow, his body frail and stiff. Challaye came to shake the *grand commandant*'s hand for the last time. Many members of the mission could not restrain their tears as four sailors carried the stretcher ashore.

Thérèse kept watch by her husband's side in a small, austere room at the French military hospital in Dakar. Doctors could do little for him, and a priest was called to perform the last rights. As his strength ebbed away, Brazzà asked Thérèse to place the photograph of their beloved son Jacques by his bed.

A few hours later, on the evening of September 14, 1905, Pierre Savorgnan de Brazzà breathed his last.

CHAPTER FIFTEEN -- HONORED SON OF FRANCE

Since his retirement from colonial service in Africa for health reasons in 1894, Charles de Chavannes had been living a quiet life in and around Lyon. Catching up with old friends, seeing to his family's financial matters, and looking after his elderly mother kept him occupied, but he found it hard to adjust to the monotony of his new life in provincial France. Challenging, difficult, and dangerous as they had been, he missed the excitement of his eleven years in French Congo.

Best man at the Brazzàs' wedding in 1895, Chavannes had corresponded frequently with Pierre and Thérèse. Like them, he had felt shock and anger at Brazzà's disgrace in 1898. He had shared in the couple's joy at the birth of their four children, and had consoled them in their sorrow at the sudden loss of little Jacques. The former "Africans" had met from time to time at occasional events in Paris, and during Pierre and Thérèse's visits with family in Lozère.

In early 1905, traveling between Rome and Paris, Brazzà had stopped to spend two days in Lyon with his old friend. They spoke of Ballay, Dolisie, Marche, and other colleagues who had passed away, and discussed their own future plans. Brazzà was considering the possibility of an official position in Tangier, Morocco. Both men were distraught at the recent reports of torture and corruption in Congo.

Reading his daily newspaper in March, Chavannes learned that Brazzà had been asked to lead the long-overdue Congo investigative mission, and that he had accepted. Chavannes wrote immediately to Brazzà to try to dissuade him. "Remember that you are now a father," wrote Chavannes. "Your first duty is to your family."

Like Thérèse, however, Brazzà's former colleague knew him well enough to surmise that the *grand commandant*'s instinctive sense of duty would lead him inexorably back to Africa. In the rush to prepare for the controversial mission, Pierre and Thérèse had not found time to respond to his letter. Chavannes remained apprehensive, and thought back to Brazzà's oft-repeated ironic phrase, "Someday Africa will be the death of me!"

After the mission's departure, Chavannes assiduously followed the progress reports that Félicien Challaye telegraphed back to the French newspaper *le Temps*. Having spent years just across the Congo River from King Leopold's totally unregulated colony, the fact that human rights abuses had now invaded French Congo did not surprise Chavannes. But like many people, he was appalled at how quickly conditions had been allowed to deteriorate. It had been only seven years since Brazzà's departure in 1898, but the torture and murder of the tribesmen, and the wholesale destruction of their homes, farms, and forests, had already reduced the population of the four regions of French Congo by thousands, perhaps millions.

In mid-September, news of Brazzà's death broke in France. Chavannes sorrowfully realized that his fears and misgivings had been correct. But now was not the time to dwell on regrets. Chavannes immediately thought of Thérèse in her bereavement, so far from home. He composed a simple, sincere message of condolence, and sent it to her by telegram at the military hospital in Dakar.

As the days went by, Chavannes tried to find out when Brazzà's remains would arrive at Marseilles, and when the train bearing his casket to Paris would pass through the Lyon train station, in case the city's notables organized a tribute to the great explorer. But no word came, and Chavannes was obliged to accompany his former colleague and friend on his last journey only in spirit.

He read that a date had been set for Brazzà's state funeral in Paris. At least France would grant her adopted son that honor.

One Saturday evening, the last day of September, Chavannes returned home to find an official telegram marked "URGENT" from Minister of the Colonies Clémentel. "Brazzà's state funeral set for Tuesday, October 3rd, 10 a.m.; would be happy if you could attend and say few words in name of friends of your former leader and friend."

Chavannes telegraphed back his acceptance, and by Monday night he had arrived at a hotel in central Paris. During the train ride he had gone over his thoughts and memories of Brazzà, and before retiring he put the words of his tribute on paper.

The next morning he crossed the Seine to the tall Basilica of Sainte Clotilde, diocesan church for the city of Paris, where the state funeral would take place. An usher escorted Chavannes to his pew at the head of a large group of Brazzà's former colleagues, including Decazes and other members of the 1882 Congo expedition, and Dr. Cureau, who had presided over Brazzà's last hours in Dakar. Directly in front of them were French government officials and representatives of the various ministries.

Glancing around the vast church, Chavannes noticed Thérèse, visibly despondent, just to the right of her husband's coffin. Her face and shoulders were covered by heavy black veils of mourning. At one point during the two-hour service, Thérèse felt unwell, and had to be brought to the sacristy to recover.

By noon, the final benediction had been given and the long funeral cortège formed in front of the basilica. The large, horse-drawn hearse was covered with palms and decorated with hangings bearing the Savorgnan di Brazzà coat of arms. Military and political officials strode beside the coffin, followed by the family, and then by Brazzà's colleagues with Chavannes at their head.

A single file of sword-bearing infantrymen escorted each side of the procession. The cortège crossed the Seine to the Place de la Concorde, passing the Ministry of the Navy where thirty years earlier, the tall, slender, enthusiastic young ensign had proposed a modest mission to explore the mysterious land that lay beyond equatorial Africa's west coast.

Advancing slowly and silently down the Rue de Rivoli and past the Louvre, the long procession seemed to stretch "as far as the eye could see," recalled Chavannes. "Every window of every building was occupied, and there was a huge crowd on either side of the avenue the entire length of the way." Some onlookers climbed the black-draped lampposts for a better view. Men removed their hats as the hearse went by.

Passing through the Place de la Bastille, the cortège continued east and came to a halt at Père-Lachaise Cemetery, where a tribune had been set up. Chavannes was shown to his seat and was told that he would give the fourth and final address.

Minister of the Colonies Étienne Clémentel, who had harbored such resentment for Brazzà's final mission and had placed so many obstacles in the investigator's path, mounted the steps of the tribune and began his grandiloquent eulogy. He spoke of the "mourning of the nation" and the "greatness of the man who has left us" in a "sudden and premature death." Brazzà was not truly deceased, he declared, because his "intention survives" among his comrades. "If he is no longer their leader, he is their model. Consecrated by his tragic end, his dream of yesterday remains the ideal of tomorrow." Brazzà's great example, concluded Clémentel, "keeps us from ever losing faith in the eternal traditions of justice and humanity that are the glory of France."

Statesman Paul Deschanel then spoke in the name of the French legislature. "Dear Brazzà," he declaimed, "You gave your magnificent, fervent soul to the most wonderful homeland ever to appear beneath the heavens. You enlarged its borders, extending the power of its genius. You were a great servant of its ideals and justice."

Senator and former colonial governor Charles-Marie Le Myre de Vilers succeeded Deschanel at the podium, where he represented the Paris Geographical Society. Decades earlier, in 1886, it was after extemporizing a toast to Le Myre's newly-assigned governorship of Madagascar that Brazzà had incurred the wrath of his naval superiors for not having this "public speech" pre-approved by the Ministry of the Navy. In 1903, Le Myre had been instrumental in the granting of Brazzà's retirement pension with the honor of "national compensation."

Now Le Myre de Vilers spoke of three explorers whose names had come to symbolize the European exploration of Africa: Livingstone, Stanley, and Brazzà. "Each one of these leaders of men," he said, "was inspired by a different principle: religious faith, a strong will, and humanity. All three are immortal."

Le Myre alluded directly to the investigative mission for which Brazzà had given his life, and the explorer's commitment "to go on site to study the reforms to be carried out in the Congo administration." He paid tribute to Thérèse, Brazzà's "valiant wife, who accompanied him on his last journeys."

He emphasized the great loss that Brazzà's death represented for all the world's explorers. After quoting the letter of condolences he had received from London's Royal Geographical Society, Le Myre concluded with a personal farewell. "Adieu, Brazzà. Rest in peace. You have gloriously accomplished your duty and served your adopted homeland."

Chavannes found it hard to control his feelings as he went to the podium to pay honor to Brazzà in the name of his many friends.

"In the midst of these sumptuous ceremonies and speeches," he began, "it is now the humble voice of a friend, deeply moved and saddened, that brings his tribute of sorrows to the dear one we have lost. During the long years that I knew Brazzà as a beloved leader and friend, many times he said that Africa would one day take his life. The prophecy has come true. Africa counts another martyr and France another hero ... but the heroism of those who fall is a terrible sacrifice for those who remain."

"One day France will remember, I hope, long after the honors of today, that Brazzà devoted to her all his intelligence, all his fortune, and his life right up to his last breath."

"... If Brazzà was without question a great man, as you have heard, he was also a man with a great heart. All those who lived the African life with him as I did, all who saw him with his family and friends, can bear witness. They know that the colossal energy that forged Brazzà's reputation was matched by infinite goodness and simplicity. ... During the 1883 expedition, when food was hard to come by, I remember seeing him invent a sudden case of exhaustion so that he could go hungry in order to let the enlisted men have a better meal. And there were so many other acts of generosity! You can easily understand the devotion and affection such qualities inspired in those around him ..."

"A great heart has stopped beating ... to him I bring a final farewell from colleagues and friends who, as I did, loved him even more than they admired him."

Chavannes' voice wavered as he concluded his tribute. "Adieu, Brazzà. Adieu in the name of those to whom you showed the path of duty, right up until the end. Farewell in the name of those to whom you gave, so simply, the touching example of your life. Farewell, Pierre, in the name of your friends. Rest in peace. May a calm, gentle image of kindness adorn the halo of glory that surrounds you."

That evening, as Chavannes dined at the Chambruns' home in Paris, Thérèse and the rest of the family expressed their gratitude for his sincere and touching speech. Pierre had left them, but he would live on in the hearts of those who loved him, and in the work that he had carried out until the last day of his life.

For despite his premature death, Brazzà had concluded the investigation. His carefully documented reports on the many interviews with African tribesmen and French administrators, and the disturbing conditions and events he had witnessed, made an irrefutable case against the French government's support of the concessionary system and its abuses.

Arriving back in France in early October 1905, Inspector of the Colonies Hoarau-Desruisseaux and the other investigators prepared to present the mission's findings to the French government. According to the established procedure, they would meet with the Minister of the Colonies who would receive their detailed report. The investigators' conclusions and suggestions would then provide the basis for much-needed reforms in the French Congo.

Much to the amazement and dismay of the widely-respected Hoarau-Desruisseaux, the well-known newspaper correspondent Félicien Challaye, and the other members of the mission, nothing of the kind took place. On the pretext of Brazzà's death, Minister Clémentel immediately dissolved the "Brazzà Mission" and replaced it with a "Congo Commission" made up of his own subordinates, many of whom had been hostile to Brazzà and his egalitarian principles. One by one, the mission investigators were called to appear before the Congo Commission where they were treated, if not as accused criminals, at the very least as suspect witnesses.

As in the days of the Dreyfus Affair a decade earlier, French newspapers began taking sides over this latest potential scandal. Throughout the last months of 1905, the liberal *l'Humanité*, *le Temps*, and *l'Aurore* accused the Ministry of the

Colonies of protecting French Congo's guilty administrators and concessionaires, while conservative journals such as *le Figaro*, at that time still generously subsidized by Leopold II of Belgium, defended Clémentel's decisions.

In February 1906, the French government published an official circular declaring amnesty for the authors of all crimes committed in French Congo. Brazzà's malevolent successor Émile Gentil was sent back to the colony as General Commissioner.

These events provoked a heated debate in the French Assembly, where representatives Gustave Rouanet, Édouard Vaillant, and the brilliant orator Jean Jaurès demanded that the Brazzà Report be published and distributed, and that reforms be enacted. Finally the question was submitted to a vote. By a margin of 345 to 167, the French National Assembly decided that the Brazzà Report, the entire record of testimonies and investigations that Pierre Savorgnan de Brazzà had given his life to assemble, would remain a "state secret" and would not be published. Ten numbered copies were printed and immediately placed in safes at the Ministry of the Colonies.

It was as if a curtain had been drawn over the Congo crimes, which would be inflicted with impunity on another generation of Africans. In 1925, traveling through the colony that Brazzà had founded, French author André Gide noted that apart from its name, little in the territory had changed. French Congo, Gabon, Ubangi-Shari, and Chad, known from 1910 to 1958 as French Equatorial Africa, still suffered under the domination of the concession companies. The tribesmen were paid less than two French francs for a kilogram of raw rubber, which was then resold in free trade areas for ten to twelve francs.

Gide saw villages abandoned for weeks while men struggled to harvest their quotas of rubber, and while women were requisitioned for road work and other forms of manual labor. Children as young as nine years old were taken away from their villages to maintain colonial lawns and gardens, and then left to find food on their own and spend the night outdoors.

Ironically, during late August 1925, Gide attended a trial in Brazzaville that was eerily similar to the Toqué-Gaud trial that Félicien Challaye had witnessed in the same city exactly twenty years earlier. A French colonial administrator named Sambry was being judged for having carried out a reign of terror over the tribesmen at a distant and isolated post. After hearing the long, disturbing list of injustices and tortures attributed to the accused, Gide noted that Sambry "got away with a year in prison." Many Africans attended the trial and heard the verdict, but their reaction was so subdued that, Gide wrote, he "could not get an idea of their opinion."

The concessionary system continued in French Equatorial Africa until 1930. Some statistics estimated that between 1911 and 1931, the colony's population of twenty million had been reduced to a mere two and a half million. This highly possible loss of more than seventeen million Africans is the equivalent of three Holocausts.

To Thérèse de Brazzà, one cruel and unnecessary death stood out from the others: the murder of her husband. Until her death in 1948 she quietly but firmly maintained that Pierre had been poisoned in Brazzaville during the last week of the investigative mission.

Photographs taken of the 53-year-old General Commissioner on the eve of his departure and during the first weeks of the mission show him looking apparently fit and healthy, and it was certainly true that in the past he had successfully recovered from many infirmities and tropical illnesses. Members of the mission observed that while Brazzà had seemed increasingly fatigued as the inspection progressed, his condition had indeed worsened abruptly during the final days in Brazzaville. No direct accusation, of course, was ever made.

Thérèse never remarried, and she devoted the rest of her life to caring for her three children. She remained entirely, perhaps obsessively, devoted to her husband's memory, purchasing the villa the family had rented in Algiers with the express intention that it be turned into a museum of his life and work after her death. On January 25, 1952, the centenary of Pierre's birth, the Brazzà Museum was officially inaugurated in Algiers, with the explorer's son Charles de Brazzà as its first curator.

Thérèse also honored Brazzà's final wish to be buried on African soil. After agreeing to the temporary interment of his remains at Père-Lachaise Cemetery in Paris after the state funeral, Thérèse had his body transferred in 1907 to Algiers, where it was received with full military honors. The *grand commandant* was buried in the European Cemetery of Algiers, on a hill overlooking the city. Thérèse asked Charles de Chavannes to compose a fitting epitaph for his dear friend. It reads in part:

> *An aggrieved France mourns the adopted son who, in her name, conquered nearly alone and unarmed an immense empire in unknown Africa, by means of his calm bravery and his invincible faith in Patience and Kindness.*
>
> *His memory is pure of human blood.*

In the 1950s and 60s, many African nations became independent from their former colonial powers. One by one, the numerous cities and towns founded by Europeans were again known by their local names, and Leopoldville, now called Kinshasa, was among the first vestiges of colonial domination to disappear.

Brazzaville, Congo, is one of the very few African capitals to retain its colonial name and it is there, in the heart of the continent that he so loved, that "the peaceful conqueror" has found his most meaningful and enduring tribute. The life he devoted to Africa, the link he forged between his adopted homeland and the mysterious land of his childhood dreams, and the hope he cherished of peace and cooperation between the nations, are remembered and honored by the Congolese people with a quiet dignity that resembles Brazzà's own.

CONCLUSION

The story of Pierre Savorgnan de Brazzà epitomizes the colonial history of Africa at its best and worst. In some ways the charismatic Franco-Italian explorer realized his goal of bringing together European and African cultures in a spirit of mutual respect and understanding. As leader of scientific expeditions, envoy to African kings, and later as colonial governor, he fought against slavery and fratricidal tribal wars and presided over a dozen years of prosperity and development in French Congo.

His well-intentioned plans, however, were shattered by the reality of a colonial system overrun with corruption and greed. His moral conscience and his single-minded opposition to the pillage of Africa by the European powers made him an embarrassment to the French establishment, which then discarded him. The mysterious continent Brazzà had explored and had hoped to enrich was ultimately humiliated and impoverished by the colonial administration he himself had introduced.

And yet, Brazzà's accomplishments were considerable. Often using his own resources to finance his missions of exploration, he and his colleagues maintained meticulous scientific and ethnological documentation in the face of some of the most challenging conditions on earth. Brazzà and his specialists noted topographic details of equatorial Africa that are present on maps printed today. They gave us drawings of plant and animal species like the DeBrazza's monkey (*Cercopithecus neglectus*) that but for their groundbreaking work might not be a part of our 21st-century zoos and encyclopedias. The fascination for daily life in tribal African societies that is so evident in Brazzà's published writings influenced many other Europeans, and encouraged the development of the new science of anthropology.

African artifacts brought back to Europe by the Brazzà expeditions helped inspire the founding of Paris' first museum of African art, and contributed largely to the western world's awareness and acceptance of African art. A year or two after Brazzà's death, these African masks, statues, and musical instruments influenced Picasso and Braque in their development of Cubism, and subsequently influenced other artistic movements, such as Surrealism.

An enigmatic and mythical figure in European history, Brazzà owes his enduring legend not to temporal power or wealth but to his extraordinary inner qualities -- an overwhelming personal charm, a canny understanding of human character, a gift for leadership, unshakeable integrity, and an indestructible optimism that some would call naïveté. During his lifetime he came to know and love Africa, and to be accepted and loved by the Africans. He charmed Europe, from the aristocrats who dined with him to the common people who read about his adventures.

Perhaps his most striking achievement is the intense devotion he inspired in those who knew him. His loyal, intelligent wife Thérèse, who never remarried. His faithful administrator Charles de Chavannes, who spoke so eloquently at Brazzà's funeral, and who turned down a medal from the French government, saying that having known Brazzà was reward enough. The young journalist Félicien Challaye, later an influential academic, whose view of French colonialism was forever altered by his experiences during Brazzà's fateful, final mission of investigation.

To the modern-day reader, Brazzà's life is a reminder that history is never so simple or so one-sided as it seems. In the long tragedy of horrifying colonial abuse and destruction, how surprising it is to come across a little-known chapter of humanity, humility, and respect for others. And how appropriate it is that Brazzà's two major tributes, the Congolese capital named for him, and the museum established in his honor in Algiers, are both on the African continent.

The world's most lasting image of Brazzà remains that of the romantic 19th-century explorer and adventurer. The handsome antique photographs of him in exotic attire assure him that role. It is paradoxical that such a profoundly independent individual has become something of an archetype of all explorers of the period. But perhaps Brazzà, like his spiritual descendent, the elegant Venetian comic-book hero Corto Maltese, represents what is best in all explorers -- a noble, courageous, attractive hero on an eternal quest into the unknown.

BRAZZÀ'S PARIS

Brazzà's apartment, 10 rue St. Florentin, 1st arrondissement (or district).
Hotel Continental (now Hotel Intercontinental), 3 rue de Castiglione, 1st arrt.
Ministry of the Colonies, Pavillon de Flore wing of the Louvre (now Louvre Museum), 1st arrt.
Cirque d'Hiver, 110 rue Amelot, 3rd arrt.
Conza, tropical clothiers (now a shoe store), 56 rue Meslay, 3rd arrt.
University of Paris / Sorbonne, rue de la Sorbonne, 5th arrt.
Ecole Préparatoire Ste Geneviève (now Institut Pasteur), rue des Postes (now rue Lhomond), 5th arrt.
la Petite Vache restaurant (now a nightclub), 66 rue Mazarine, 6th arrt.
Hotel de Bade (now another hotel), 44 rue Jacob, 6th arrt.
Paris Geographical Society, 184 bd. St Germain, 6th arrt.
Institut de France (the "French Academy"), 23 quai de Conti, 6th arrt.
Bon Marché department store, 22 rue de Sèvres, 7th arrt.
Palace of the Legion of Honor, 1 rue de la Légion

d'Honneur, 7th arrt.
National Assembly, Place du Palais Bourbon, 7th arrt.
Ministry of Foreign Affairs, quai d'Orsay, 7th arrt.
Brazzà's wedding, Bourbon-Condé chapel, 12 rue Monsieur, 7th arrt.
Brazzà's funeral, Ste Clotilde Basilica, rue Las Cases, 7th arrt.
Residence of Brazzà's cousin, the Duchess Fitz-James, 118 rue du Faubourg Saint Honoré, 8th arrt.
Chambrun family home, 23 rue Matignon (now avenue Matignon), 8th arrt.
Ministry of the Navy, 2 rue Royale, 8th arrt.
Gare du Nord train station, 10th arrt.
Gare de Lyon train station, 12th arrt.
Gare d'Orléans (now Gare d'Austerlitz) train station, 13th arrt.

NOTES

Nearly all of the quotations I have used are from French or Italian sources, and have been translated by me. Sources are given for direct quotations, which are identified by their closing words, and for a few other passages about which I suggest complementary information. Works are identified by author, or by author and title. Full information on all works cited can be found in the Bibliography.

CHAPTER ONE -- THE COUNT OF BRAZZÀ
page
2 "*because he loved her*" Gabriel Hanotaux, *Pour le Congo francais*, quoted in Autin, p.143
2 "*shake his hand and kiss it*" Attilio Pecile in Brazzà, *Conférences et lettres*, p. 282.
2 "*what he is saying*" Charles de Chavannes, *Avec Brazza*, p 81.
3 "*in the last twenty years*" "Ultor", pp. 4, 5.
9 "*I could have introduced you*" Sich, pp. 17, 18.

CHAPTER TWO -- LE CARTAHU
23 *but his enthusiasm remained* Brazzà recounts his conversations and experiences aboard the *Vénus* in *Au Coeur de l'Afrique*, pp. 24, 25.

235

24   "*industrious and peaceful*" Alfred Marche, quoted in Broc, p. 224.

CHAPTER FOUR -- THE FATHER OF SLAVES
42   *for supernatural powers* Brazzà describes the events of the Ogoway Mission, including his meetings with Renoke, in Au Coeur de l'Afrique, pp. 40, 41.
46   "*brandy from the coast*" Sich, pp. 37, 38.
46   "*not an easy task*" Brazzà, Conférences et lettres, pp. 69, 70.
47   "*insulate ourselves*" ibid., p 66.
49   "*entering their territory*" Sich, p. 46.
53   "*flagpole will be free*" ibid., p. 48.
54   "*without warming your body*" Brazzà, Conférences et lettres, p. 77.
55   "*phosphorescent magnesium*" Sich, p. 51.
56   "*your tribes, will decide*" Brazzà, Au Coeur de l'Afrique, pp. 74, 75.

CHAPTER FIVE -- THE BAREFOOT CONQUEROR
60   "*He has five toes!*" Brazzà recounts this incident in Au Coeur de l'Afrique, p. 76.
62   "*Nonsense*" Sich, pp. 56, 57.
68   "*one by his uncle*" ibid., pp. 59, 60.
68   "*Peace be with you*" Brazzà, Au Coeur de l'Afrique, p. 121.
69   "*Booué! Booué!*" ibid., p. 125.
74   "*Not at all*" Sich, pp.62, 63.
77   "*that come from your country*" Brazzà, Au Coeur de l'Afrique, p. 186.
78   "*tribes along its banks*" Brazzà, Conférences et lettres, pp. 35.
80   "*victory banquet*" ibid., pp. 43, 44.
80   "*raining all around him*" Sich, p. 71.

CHAPTER SIX -- THE EXPLORER
89   "*Africa's most intrepid explorer*" Brazzà, Conférences et lettres, p. 174.
93   "*brilliant career I can offer you?*" Brazzà's meeting with Leopold II is described in Autin, p. 57, and in Sich, p. 82.

CHAPTER SEVEN -- THE CHALLENGER
98   "*in west central Africa*" Sich, p. 91.
99   "*guide you as his friend*" Brazzà, Conférences et lettres, p. 150.
101   "*your interests as to ours*" ibid., p. 155.

102	*"as men of peace"* ibid., p. 157.
103	*"than we were treated"* ibid., p. 159.
104	*"worthy of my trust"* ibid., pp. 159, 160.
104	*"we belong to him"* ibid., p. 162
104	*"all those beneath it"* ibid., p. 162
105	*"as well as ours"* ibid., pp. 165, 166.
105	*"from us a second time"* ibid., pp. 165, 166.
106	*"cartridges and gunpowder"* ibid., p. 167.
109	*"position of this gentleman"* Stanley, *The Congo and the Founding of its Free State*, vol. I, p. 231.

CHAPTER EIGHT -- THE TOAST OF PARIS

113	*"frank and manly"* Stanley, *The Congo and the Founding of its Free State*, vol. I, p. 292.
116	*"honor of the French flag"* Witte, p. 18.
117	*"patriotic above all"* Brazzà, *Conférences et lettres*, p. 178.
118	"Commandant 'Get the hell out of here'" This is my translation of the vulgar French expression "Commandant 'Fous-moi le camp,'" quoted in Autin, p. 84.
118	*"coming to work for us"* Leopold II to Brazzà, quoted in Brazzà, *Conférences et lettres*, p. 174.
119	*"cheapest means possible"* Sich, p. 119.
121	*"to civilization and to France"* Autin, p. 77.
122	*"not the guilty party"* Brazzà, *Conférences et lettres*, p. 208.
124	*"I will kill you tonight"* Both versions are quoted in Brokken, pp. 190, 191.
125	*"pristine helplessness and savagery"* Pakenham, pp. 159, 160.
126	*"each under its own flag"* Brokken, p. 191.
126	"All I offer in return is this" Chambrun, p. 124.

CHAPTER NINE -- THE GENERAL COMMISSIONER

132	*"what can I do for you?"* The conversations between Brazzà and Chavannes are taken from Chavannes' excellent memoir, *Avec Brazzà*, pp. 15-18.
135	*"the work of France"* Chambrun, p. 130.
135	*"we were hiring ambassadors?"* Sich, p. 130.
143	*"abstain from commentary"* Autin, p. 99.

143   *"at it again in January"* ibid., p. 99.
144   *"sobering experience"* Sich, pp. 137, 138.
144   *"Look at his gifts"* Autin, p. 104.

CHAPTER TEN -- THE DIPLOMAT

150   *fourteen million francs a year* Brazzà discusses the results of his first three missions in Congoon pp. 255-267 of *Conférences et lettres*. He quotes the figure of fourteen million francs from Louis Vignon, *Les Colonies françaises* (Paris: Guillaumin, 1886).

153   *Cirque d'Hiver* The interior and exterior of this attractive Parisian landmark can be admired in the 1956 Carol Reed film *Trapeze*, starring Burt Lancaster and Tony Curtis.

154   *"everything in one blow"* The minutes of the Paris Geographical Society's special session, including the full text of Brazzà's speech and Ferdinand de Lesseps' closing remarks, was published soon after the event. See Bibliography section **I.**, Savorgnan de Brazzà, *Exposé présenté dans la séance générale extraordinaire tenue au Cirque d'Hiver, le 21 janvier 1886*.

156   *"this new African France"* Article in *la Patrie*, January 22, 1886, quoted in Autin, p. 132.

156   *"refuse him nothing"* Chavannes, *Avec Brazza*, p. 363.

156   *"warning was not sufficient"* Vice-Admiral Aubé to Brazzà, quoted in Autin, p.133.

157   *"formerly mysterious lands"* Autin, p. 136.

CHAPTER ELEVEN -- ROCAMAMBO

159   *"geographical exploration"* Joseph Conrad in *Last Essays*, quoted in the Introduction to *Heart of Darkness*, p. xxiii.

162   *"begin everything again slowly"* Brazzà to Chavannes, quoted in Sich, pp. 149, 150.

168   *"left in peace"* Albert Dolisie to Brazzà, April 8, 1890, reproduced in Rabut, p. 58.

168   *"evil white man"* Autin, p. 168.

170   *"outfit and hairstyle"* Madame d'Abbadie to Thérèse de Chambrun, March 10, 1895, Brazzà Papers.

171   *"That was she"* Madame d'Abbadie to Brazzà, March 19, 1895, Brazzà Papers.

171   *"make you my wife"* Brazzà to Thérèse de Brazzà, April 5, 1899, Brazzà Papers.

CHAPTER TWELVE -- THE BRIDEGROOM

173   *"please put on a little powder!"* Madame d'Abbadie to Thérèse de Chambrun, April 14, 1895, Brazzà Papers.

173   *"white dress looked wonderful"* Madame d'Abbadie to Thérèse de Chambrun, April 16, 1895, Brazzà Papers.

173   *"wouldn't have come to stay here"* Brazzà to Thérèse de Chambrun, May 20, 1895, Brazzà Papers.

174   *"nephew and adopted son"* Aldebert de Chambrun to Brazzà, July 1, 1895, Brazzà Papers.

175   *"And I did"* Brazzà quoted in *Le Vélo*, October 1895, quoted in Autin, p. 196.

178   *"negrophile politics"* Autin, p. 201.

180   *on a budget of 3,700,000* These figures are quoted from Autin, p. 205

182   *"a new African France"* Autin, p. 212.

CHAPTER THIRTEEN -- THE FATHER

191   *"to enjoy his own life"* Brazzà to Chavannes, January 2, 1904, Brazzà Papers.

194   *"Blacks from making trouble"* Challaye, p. 63.

CHAPTER FOURTEEN -- THE INVESTIGATOR

200   *"exploitation of a subjugated people"* Challaye, p. 24.

201   *"chosen me for this investigation"* Autin, p. 241.

202   *"for your personal safety"* Humbert to Brazzà, March 4, 1905, Brazzà Papers.

203   *"without clearing his head"* Superville to Emile Gentil, March 25, 1905, quoted in Autin, p. 242.

205   *"around his neck"* Challaye, p. 49. Along with the reports Brazzà telegraphed back to French government officials in Paris, Félicien Challaye's meticulous notes are the most reliable source of information on the events of

Brazzà's final mission.
206 *"more criticism than praise"* Witte, p. 316.
207 *"a calumny"* ibid., p. 318.
207 *"Monsieur de Brazza"* Autin, p. 245.
208 *"a dream fulfilled"* Pakenham, p. 635.
208 *"There's no rubber"* Challaye, pp. 51, 52.
210 *"a new form of slavery"* ibid., p. 70.
213 *"just to keep business going"* Challaye, p. 61. All quotes from the Toqué-Gaud trial are taken from Challaye's account.
215 *"make you turn nigger"* Challaye, p. 67.
216 *"a bit more reserved"* Dr. T. Rossi-Doria to the Count and Countess Savorgnan de Brazzà, August 13, 1905, Brazzà Papers.

CHAPTER FIFTEEN -- HONORED SON OF FRANCE
219 *"duty is to your family"* Chavannes to Brazzà, quoted in Chavannes, Le Congo français, p. 383. My principal source for this chapter is Chavannes' detailed memoir.
220 *"former leader and friend"* Etienne Clémentel to Charles de Chavannes, in Chavannes, Le Congo français, p. 385.
221 *"entire length of the way"* Chavannes, Le Congo français, p.386.
222 *"the glory of France"* ibid., p. 387.
222 *"its ideals and justice"* ibid., p. 388.
223 *"served your adopted homeland"* ibid., p. 388.
224 *"glory that surrounds you"* ibid., pp. 388-390.
227 *"an idea of their opinion"* Gide, p. 27.
228 *"His memory is pure of human blood"* Epitaph written by Charles de Chavannes, quoted in Chavannes, Le Congo français, p. 394.

ABOUT THE RESEARCH

My first sources of information on Brazzà were the Congolese people I met during my 18-month stay in Brazzaville in the 1980s. Their words, "We will never change the name of Brazzaville," still echo in my mind. But apart from these conversations, I found little information on the explorer in Congo. All relevant colonial files had been returned to France at the time of Congolese independence in 1960.

My serious research began years later with Brazzà's own writings, and the half-dozen out-of-print French books devoted to him, particularly the interesting biographies by Jean Autin and Marc Sich. The superlative research in the Brunschwig and Coquery-Vidrovitch works helped me to complete my basic knowledge of Brazzà's life and career, and this knowledge was enriched by the personal reminiscences of Chavannes, Challaye, and Chambrun. As I became more familiar with my subject, I was able to formulate questions about various aspects of the French and Italian societies that produced the explorer, and about the European colonial systems which framed his life's work. My bibliography expanded accordingly.

The welcome I received from Brazzà's grandnephew, Dr. Detalmo Pirzio-Biroli, at the Castello di Brazzà in northern Italy, was an inestimable asset to my endeavor. It was through Detalmo, for example, that I was able to determine that Brazzà had indeed been born in Castel Gandolfo, not in Rome or elsewhere, as is commonly reported. Detalmo also shared memories of his conversations with Brazzà's widow, Thérèse, in her later years. Lucia Pirzio-Biroli, Brazzà's American great-grandniece, further increased my knowledge of the explorer's family history.

Following Brazzà's footsteps in Paris was another of the more enjoyable and inspiring aspects of the research. Some of the lodgings, restaurants, shops, schools, and institutes he frequented still exist; many do not. Several of the streets have new names. But thanks to the wealth of documentation available on the history of Paris, including the excellent exhibits at the Musée Carnavalet, and France's invaluable and painstaking attention to its architectural heritage, I was able to determine, and in most cases visit, the scenes of all the Parisian events in Brazzà's life.

Certainly the most exciting part of the research was being able to handle and read letters written by Brazzà himself, conserved at France's Archives d'Outre-Mer (Overseas, or Colonial, Archives) in Aix-en-Provence. Archival research is, of course, very different from library research. It is much more challenging and more rewarding. France's various archives have done an excellent job of preserving and cataloguing precious documents like these.

Lastly, I learned much about 19th-century daily life, customs, and fashions in Europe through the often-overlooked but extremely helpful resources of popular magazines of the day, handbills, antique postcards, and other ephemera sold at the *bouquiniste* stalls along the Seine.

BIBLIOGRAPHY

I. Life of Pierre Savorgnan de Brazzà

ARNAUT, Robert.
    Sur les traces de Stanley et Brazza. Paris: Mercure de France, 1989.

AUTIN, Jean.
    Pierre Savorgnan de Brazza: un prophète du Tiers Monde. Paris: Perrin, 1985.

BALDISSERA, Caterina, ed.
    Pietro Savorgnan di Brazzà, esploratore friulano. [Catalogue of a 1982 exhibit of family memorabilia]. Passariano: Regione Autonoma Friuli-Venezia Giulia, 1982.

BALLIF, Noël.
    Le Congo. Paris: Karthala, 1993.

BRITSCH, Amédée.
    Histoire de la dernière mission Brazza. Paris: Davy, 1906.
    Pour le Congo français. La dernière mission Brazza, d'après le régistre de correspondance inédit de P. Savorgnan de Brazza. Paris: L. de Soye et fils, 1906.

BRUNSCHWIG, Henri.
    Brazza explorateur: L'Ogooué, 1875-79. Paris: Mouton, 1966.
    Brazza explorateur: Les traités Makoko, 1880-82. Paris: Mouton, 1972.

CASTRIES, Duc de.
    Les Rencontres de Stanley, essai historique. Paris: Editions France Empire, 1993.

CHALLAYE, Félicien.
> *Un livre noir du colonialisme: Souvenirs sur la colonisation.* Reprint of the 1935 edition, with additional documents and a preface by Michel Dreyfus. Paris: Les Nuits rouges, 1998.

CHAMBRUN, [Général] Aldebert de.
> *Brazza.* Paris: Plon, 1930.
> *Le Musée Savorgnan de Brazza, 25 janvier 1852 - 25 janvier 1952, à Alger.* Alger: Imprimerie officielle, 1952.

CHAVANNES, Charles de.
> *Mission de Brazza au Congo. Exposé sommaire du voyage dans l'Ouest africain présenté le 21 février 1886 à la Société de Géographie de Lyon.* Lyon: Mougin-Rusand, 1886.
> *Les Origines de l'Afrique équatoriale française. I: Avec Brazza: Souvenirs de la mission de l'Ouest africain (mars 1883 - janvier 1886).* Paris: Plon, 1936.
> *Les Origines de l'Afrique équatoriale française. II: Le Congo français. Ma collaboration avec Brazza (1886-1894), nos relations jusqu'à sa mort (1905).* With a preface by Thérèse de Brazza. Paris: Plon, 1937.
> *Pour le cinquantenaire de Brazzaville* with *L'Episode du sergent Malamine.* Paris: Editions du Comité de l'Afrique française, 1931.

COQUERY-VIDROVITCH, Catherine.
> *Brazza et la prise de possession du Congo 1883-1885.* 2 vols. Paris: E. P. H. E., 1969.

CRISENOY, Maria de.
> *Le Héros du Congo: Pierre Savorgnan de Brazza.* With a preface by Thérèse de Brazza. Paris: Spes, 1940.

DUTREUIL DE RHINS, Jules-Léon.
> *Mission de Brazza dans l'Ouest africain.* Bordeaux: Gounouilhou, 1884.

MALO, Henri.
> *A l'enseigne de la Petite Vache.* Paris: Nouvelle France, 1946.

MARAN, René.
> *Brazza et la fondation de l'Afrique Equatoriale Française.* Paris: Dauphin, 1941.

NEUVILLE, Didier, and Charles BREARD.
> *Les voyages de Savorgnan de Brazza: Ogôoué et Congo (1875-1882).* Paris: Berger-Levrault, 1884.

NWOYE, Rosaline Eradepa.
> *The Public Image of Pierre Savorgnan de Brazzà and the Establishment of French Imperialism in the Congo, 1875-1885.* Aberdeen: Aberdeen Univ. African Studies Group, 1981.

RABUT, Elisabeth.
> *Brazza, commissaire général: le Congo français 1886-1897.* Paris: Editions EHESS, 1989.

REYNIER, Marguerite, and Félix BROUTET.
> *Quelques Français, hommes de science et d'action.* Paris: Bourrelier, 1944.

SAVORGNAN DE BRAZZÀ, Marthe.
> *Savorgnan de Brazza, conquérant pacifique.* Paris: Je sers, 1943.

SAVORGNAN DE BRAZZÀ, Pierre.
> *Au coeur de l'Afrique: Vers la source des grands fleuves, 1875-1887.* Paris: Payot, 1994.
>
> *Conférences et lettres sur ses trois explorations dans l'ouest africain de 1875 à 1886.* Ed. Napoléon Ney. Facsimile of the 1887 edition with an introduction by Célestin Goma-Foutou. Brazzaville: Editions Bantoues, 1984.
>
> *Expédition sur les cours supérieurs de l'Ogooué, de l'Alima et de la Licona.* Paris: Delagrave, 1879.
>
> *Exposé présenté dans la séance générale extraordinaire tenue au Cirque d'Hiver, le 21 janvier 1886.* Paris: Société de Géographie, 1886.
>
> *Lettre à M. Paul Bourde, écrite de Brazzaville, à la veille de son retour en France, sur les impressions et les conclusions de l'enquête qu'il vient de terminer au Congo (24 août 1905).* Paris: L. de Soye, 1906.

SICH, Marc.
> *Pierre Savorgnan de Brazza.* Paris: J.C. Lattès, 1992.

"ULTOR".
> *Deux Opinions sur M Savorgnan de Brazza.* Saint-Ouen: imprimerie de Saint-Ouen, 1896.

WEST, Richard.
    Congo. New York: Holt, Rinehart and Winston, 1972.

II. History of the Savorgnan di Brazzà Family and the Friuli Region

MUIR, Edward.
    Mad Blood Stirring: Vendettas and Factions in Friuli during the Renaissance. Baltimore & London: Johns Hopkins Univ. Press, 1993.

ROSSI-DORIA, Manlio.
    La gioia tranquilla del ricordo. Bologna: Soc. ed. il Mulino, 1991.

SAVORGNAN DI BRAZZÀ, Alvise.
    "Maladetti Savorgnan", mille anni di simbiosi con Udine. Udine: A.G.F., 1983.

III. Social, Political, and Historical Background of French Colonialism

AGERON, Charles-Robert.
    La décolonisation française. Paris: A. Colin, 1991.
    France coloniale ou parti colonial? Paris: P. U. F., 1978.

ASCHERSON, Neal.
    The King Incorporated: Leopold II in the Age of Trusts. New York: Doubleday, 1964.

BARRACLOUGH, Geoffrey.
    An Introduction to Contemporary History. Harmondsworth, England: Penguin, 1982.

BETTS, Raymond F.
    France and Decolonisation, 1900-1960. Basingstoke: Macmillan, 1991.
    Tricouleur: the French Overseas Empire. London: Gordon/Cremonesi, 1978.

BIRNBAUM, Pierre.
    L'Affaire Dreyfus: la république en péril. Paris: Gallimard, 1994.

BOUCHE, Denise.
    Histoire de la colonisation française. Tome second: Flux et reflux (1815-1962). Paris: Fayard, 1991.

BOURGIN, Georges.
    La Commune. Paris: P. U. F., 1980.
BUISINE, Alain.
    Pierre Loti: l'écrivain et son double. Paris: Tallandier, 1998.
EMERSON, Barbara.
    Leopold II of the Belgians: King of Colonialism. New York: St. Martin's Press, 1979.
FERRO, Marc.
    Histoire des colonisations: des conquêtes aux indépendances, XIIIe – XXe siècle. Paris: Seuil, 1994.
FORBATH, Peter.
    The River Congo: The discovery, exploration, and exploitation of the world's most dramatic river. Boston: Houghton Mifflin, 1991.
GIRARDET, Raoul.
    L'Idée coloniale en France: de 1871 à 1962. Paris: Hachette, 1979.
GUILLAUME, Pierre.
    Le Monde colonial, XIXe - XXe siècle. Paris: Armand Colin, 1974.
GUILLEMINAULT, Gilbert.
    Le Roman vrai de la IIIe et de la IVe République, 1870-1958. Volume I: 1870-1918. Paris: Laffont, 1991.
GUILLEMOT, Marcel.
    Notice sur le Congo français. Exposition universelle de 1900, Colonies françaises. Paris, 1900.
HANOTAUX, Gabriel.
    Mon temps. Volume II: La Troisième République: Gambetta et Jules Ferry. Paris: Plon, 1938.
KLOTCHKOFF, Jean-Claude.
    Le Congo aujourd'hui. Paris: Editions J.A., 1987.
LANCHER, M. A.
    Les Richesses africaines et les moyens de les acquérir. Paris: Aimé, 1886.
LEBON, André.
    La Politique de la France en Afrique, 1896-1898, mission Marchand, Niger, Madagascar. Paris: Plon-Nourrit, 1901.

LEJEUNE, Dominique.
    La France des débuts de la IIIe République 1870-1896. Paris: Armand Colin, 1994.
LE TARGAT, François.
    A la recherche de Pierre Loti. Paris: Seghers, 1974.
LUGAN, Bernard.
    Afrique, bilan de la décolonisation. Paris: Perrin, 1991.
MOOREHEAD, Alan.
    The White Nile. New York: Harper & Row, 1971.
MURPHY, Agnes.
    The Ideology of French Imperialism 1871-1881. Washington: The Catholic University of America Press, 1948.
NOUSCHI, A. and A. OLIVESI,
    La France de 1848 à 1914. Paris: Fernand Nathan, 1981.
PAKENHAM, Thomas.
    The Scramble for Africa: White Man's Conquest of the Dark Continent from 1876 to 1912. New York: Avon Books, 1991.
PIGAFETTA, Filippo.
    A Report of the Kingdom of Congo and of the Surrounding Countries, Drawn out of the Writings and Discourses of the Portuguese Duarte Lopez. Trans. M. Hutchinson. Facsimile of the 1881 edition. London: Frank Cass, 1970.
PRADALIÉ, Georges.
    Le Second Empire. Paris: P. U. F., 1974.
READER, John.
    Africa: A Biography of the Continent. London: Hamish Hamilton, 1997.
REMY, Mylène.
    Le Gabon aujourd'hui. Paris: Editions du Jaguar, 1996.
RÉUNION DES MUSÉES NATIONAUX.
    Le Temps Toulouse Lautrec. Paris: Textuel, 1991.
SAWYER, Roger.
    Casement: The Flawed Hero. London: Routledge & Kegan Paul, 1984.

IV. Life in French Colonial Africa

ALLEGRET, Marc.
    Carnets du Congo: Voyage avec Gide. Paris: C.N.R.S., 1987.
AUGOUARD, [Monseigneur] Prosper.
    28 Années au Congo: Lettres de Monseigneur Augouard. 2 vols. Poitiers: S. F. I. L., 1905.
BERLIOUX, E.-F.
    Les anciennes explorations et les futures découvertes de l'Afrique centrale. Lyon: Perrin & Marinet, 1879.
BIERMAN, John.
    Dark Safari: The Life Behind the Legend of Henry Morton Stanley. London: Hodder & Stoughton, 1990.
BROC, Numa.
    Dictionnaire illustré des explorateurs et grands voyageurs français du XIXe siècle. Tome I: Afrique. Paris: Editions du C.T.H.S., 1988.
BROKKEN, Jan.
    The Rainbird: A Central African Journey. Trans. Sam Garrett. Hawthorn, Australia: Lonely Planet, 1997.
BRUNSCHWIG, Henri.
    Noirs et blancs dans l'Afrique noire française ou comment le colonisé devient colonisateur. Paris: Flammarion, 1982.
    Le Partage de l'Afrique noire. Paris: Flammarion, 1993.
BURTON, [Sir] Richard Francis.
    Wanderings in West Africa from Liverpool to Fernando Po. London: Tinsley, 1863.
    Wit and Wisdom from West Africa, or a Book of Proverbial Philosophy, Idioms, Enigmas, and Laconisms. London: Tinsley, 1865.
CASEMENT, Roger.
    The Black Diaries: An Account of Roger Casement's Life and Times with a Collection of his Diaries and Public Writings. Eds. Peter Singleton-Gates and Maurice Girodias. New York: Grove Press, 1959.

CONRAD, Joseph.
> *Heart of Darkness* with *The Congo Diary*. Ed. with an introduction and notes by Robert Hampson. London: Penguin, 1995.

COQUERY-VIDROVITCH, Catherine.
> *Le Congo au temps des grandes compagnies concessionnaires: 1898-1930.* Paris: Mouton, 1972.

DU CHAILLU, Paul Belloni.
> *Explorations and Adventures in Equatorial Africa.* Reprint of the 1861 edition. New York: Negro Universities Press, 1969.

GIDE, André.
> *Voyage au Congo*, suivi de *Le retour du Tchad*. Paris: Gallimard, 1927.

HOCHSCHILD, Adam.
> *King Leopold's Ghost: A Story of Greed, Terror, and Heroism in Colonial Africa.* New York: Houghton Mifflin, 1998.

JOHNSTON, [Sir] Harry.
> *George Grenfell and the Congo.* New York: Negro Universities Press, 1969.

KINGSLEY, Mary Henrietta.
> *Congo français, Corisco and Cameroons.* London: Macmillan, 1897.

LANDEROIN, Moïse-Augustin.
> *Mission Congo-Nil, mission Marchand: carnets de route.* Paris: L'Harmattan, 1996.

LEIRIS, Michel.
> *Miroir de l'Afrique.* Paris: Gallimard, 1996.

LIVINGSTONE, David.
> *Livingstone's Private Journal, 1851-1853.* Ed. I. Schapera. London: Chatto & Windus, 1960.
>
> *Livingstone's African Journal, 1853-1856.* Ed. I. Schapera. 2 vols. London: Chatto & Windus, 1963.
>
> *The Last Journals of David Livingstone in Central Africa from 1865 to his death.* Ed. Horace Waller. 2 vols. London: J. Murray, 1874.

LIVINGSTONE, David and Charles.
> *Narrative of an Expedition to the Zambesi and its Tributaries, and of the Discovery of the Lakes Shirwa and Nyassa, 1858-1864.* London, J. Murray, 1865.

LIVRE D'OR DU CENTENAIRE DE BRAZZAVILLE.
> Under the auspices of the People's Republic of the Congo. Brazzaville: Publi-Congo, 1980.

M'BOKOLO, Elikia.
> *Afrique noire. Tome II: XIXe et XXe siècles: Histoire et civilisations.* Paris: Mouton, 1981.

METEGUE N'NAH, Nicolas.
> *Domination coloniale au Gabon, la résistance d'un peuple (1839-1960). Tome I: Les combattants de la première heure (1839-1920).* Paris: L'Harmattan, 1981.

MICHEL, Marc.
> *La Mission Marchand, 1895-1899.* Paris: Mouton, 1972.

MOREL, Edmund Dene.
> *The British Case in French Congo: the Story of a Great Injustice, its Causes and its Lessons.* London: Heinemann, 1903.
> *Red Rubber: the Story of the Rubber Slave Trade Flourishing on the Congo in the Year of Grace 1906.* London: T. F. Unwin, 1907.

SCHWEITZER, Albert.
> *African Notebook.* Trans. C. E. B. Russell. Bloomington: Indiana Univ. Press, 1965.

STANLEY, Henry Morton.
> *The Autobiography of sir Henry Morton Stanley, edited by his wife, Dorothy Stanley.* London: Low, Marston and Co., 1909.
> *The Congo and the Founding of its Free State: A Story of Work and Exploration.* 2 vols. London: Low, Marston, Searle and Rivington, 1885.
> *How I Found Livingstone: Travels, Adventures and Discoveries in Central Africa, Including Four Months' Residence with Dr. Livingstone.* London: Low, Marston, Low and Searle, 1872.
> *In Darkest Africa, or the Quest, Rescue and Retreat of Emin, Governor of Equatoria.* 2 vols. London: Low, Marston,

Low and Searle, 1890.

Through the Dark Continent; or The Sources of the Nile Around the Great Lakes of Equatorial Africa and Down the Livingstone River to the Atlantic Ocean. 2 vols. London: Low, Marston, Low and Searle, 1878.

TOQUÉ, Georges.
Les Massacres du Congo: la terre qui ment, la terre qui tue. Paris: L'Harmattan, 1996.

UZÈS, Marie-Adrienne de Rochechouart-Mortemart, duchesse d'.
Le Voyage de mon fils au Congo. Paris: Plon, 1894.

WITTE, [Baron] Jehan de.
Monseigneur Augouard. Sa vie, ses notes de voyage et sa correspondance. With an Introduction by Mgr. Alexandre Le Roy. Paris: Émile-Paul Frères, 1924.

YOUNGS, Tim.
Travellers in Africa: British Travelogues, 1850-1900. Manchester: Manchester Univ. Press, 1994.

V. History of the City of Paris

AMIOT, Rodolphe.
Si Paris m'était conté. Paris: Contact Communication, 2000.

CARMONA, Michel.
Haussmann. Paris: Fayard, 2000.

COLE, Robert.
A Traveller's History of Paris. Gloucestershire: Windrush Press, 1997.

ERNOULT, Jean.
La Maison Mère de la Congrégation du Saint-Esprit. Paris: Congrégation du Saint-Esprit, 1997.

LE GUIDE DU PROMENEUR.
Various authors. Volumes 1-20 (*1er au 20e arrondissements*). Paris: Parigramme, 1993-97.

JORDAN, David P.
Transforming Paris: The Life and Labors of Baron Haussmann. New York: The Free Press, 1995.

VIGUIER, Odile.
Mémento d'histoire de Paris. Paris: Roudil, 1998.

VI. Periodicals

Unless otherwise noted, all journals listed below were published in Paris.

L'Aurore
Bulletin de la Société de Géographie [de Paris] and *Comptes rendus des séances*
Le Correspondant
> A detailed article by Amédée Britsch describing the final mission, based on Brazzà's unpublished correspondence during the investigation, appeared on January 10, 1906. It was published the same year as *Pour le Congo français: La dernière mission Brazza...* (see section I. above).

Le Figaro
> Articles particularly unfavorable to Brazzà appeared on March 25, 1897, and August 8, 1897.

L'Humanité
L'Illustration
> An illustrated report of Brazzà's death in Senegal and his state funeral in France appeared on October 7, 1905.

Journal des Débats
Journal des Voyages
> Descriptions of Brazzà's travels include "Les Voyages de Savorgnan de Brazza" by Adolphe Burdo, pp. 401-403, in issue no. 442, December 27, 1885.

Le Matin
> One of the first reports of the Toqué-Gaud Scandal appeared on February 16, 1905.

Le Mouvement géographique (Brussels)

La Patrie
    A review of Brazzà's successful speech at the Cirque d'hiver appeared on January 22, 1886.
Le Petit Journal
La Politique coloniale
    One of several articles attacking Brazzà appeared on January 9, 1897.
La Revue des deux mondes
La Revue Scientifique
    A review of the Muséum d'Histoire Naturelle's exhibition of African artifacts brought back by Brazzà's third mission appeared on July 1, 1885.
Le Temps
The Times (London)
    Articles discussing the confrontation between Brazzà and Stanley in Paris appeared on October 20 & 21, 1882.
Le Tour du Monde
    Among many references to Brazzà is the serialization of his memoir of the Ogoway Mission, "Voyages dans l'Ouest Africain" in vol. 54 (1887), pp. 289-304, 305-320, 321-336, and vol. 56 (1888), pp. 1-16, 17-32, 33-48, 49-64. The memoir was published in 1992 and 1994 as *Au Coeur de l'Afrique* (see section **I.** above).
Le Vélo

VII. Unpublished Sources

Official and Personal Papers of Pierre Savorgnan de Brazzà, Centre des Archives d'Outre-Mer, Aix-en-Provence, France.
Savorgnan di Brazzà Family Archives, Castello di Brazzà, S. Margherita (Udine), Italy.
Dossier Pierre Savorgnan de Brazzà, Ordre de la Légion d'Honneur, Archives Nationales de France, Paris.
Dossier Pierre Savorgnan de Brazzà, Archives du Ministère de la Marine, Paris.
Archives of the Société Géographique de Paris, Département des Cartes et Plans, Bibliothèque Nationale de France (Richelieu site),

Paris.

Département des Estampes et Photographies, Bibliothèque Nationale de France (Richelieu site), Paris.

Official Papers of Charles de Chavannes, Bibliothèque Nationale de France (Richelieu site), Paris.

Printed in Great Britain
by Amazon.co.uk, Ltd.,
Marston Gate.